IBRARY
NUE
330
D1199909

EASY-TO-BUILD OUTDOOR PROJECTS

29 PROJECTS FOR YOUR YARD AND GARDEN

FROM THE EDITORS OF POPULAR WOODWORKING

POPULAR WOODWORKING BOOKS
CINCINNATI, OHIO
www.popularwoodworking.com

684.18
Eq79
9

Table of Contents

Seating

Tables

Houses

More

Introduction

"Outdoor" can mean something different to each individual. My outdoor may be a wooden deck overlooking a lake. Your outdoor may be 20 acres of wooded land, while another person's outdoor may be the high dessert with a yard of stone and cactus. It's not only the topography that changes, but when the outdoor can be enjoyed — it's a big country, and our seasons dictate when we can appreciate nature one-on-one.

Beyond these variables, we humans do have an affinity for the great outdoors. Interesting that civilization seems to be built on creating ways to separate us from nature (bigger houses, air conditioning and technological advances to keep us inside and busy), but we still retain our love for the outdoors, enough so that many of our vacations are built around getting back to nature and viewing the natural world. And that's why we continue to value the "outdoor" that is right in our own backyard. While we all enjoy nature, we also tend to want to adapt it for our personal use, and that's where the projects in this book come in.

We've collected a selection of projects, ranging from seating to bird feeders, with a few other odds and ends tossed in. There are no decks or pergolas ... that's a different book. Most of the projects require significantly less time, money and experience to build than a traditional furniture project allowing you more time to enjoy the finished work — and your outdoors. All the projects include detailed instruction, illustrations and material cutting lists to build the projects as shown, though we always encourage personalization. Don't hesitate to make changes. That's what building your own is all about.

We hope you enjoy the book, enjoy the projects (both the building and the using) and enjoy the great outdoors!

—DAVID THIEL, EDITOR

Garden Swing

BY DAVID THIEL

When lunch is served at the garden swing, simply pop up the center section of the seat to turn it into a handy built-in table.

Nothing says summer like a glass of lemonade, relaxing in the shade and hoping to catch a breeze—or creating your own by giving your swing a kick. Of course, I always get so comfortable I'm looking for a place to put my drink down and close my eyes. Now I've got a swing designed to help. Integrated into the seat is a simple pop-up table that sits level to the ground while the swing keeps your back at a comfortable angle.

Start the project by heading to the lumber yard. The six-foot swing as shown required one 2x8, one 2x6, five 2x4s, and 10 1x4s all in eight-foot lengths. I chose western red cedar because it's a durable, lightweight, outdoor wood and is less expensive than redwood. At Midwest prices, the lumber cost about $120.

Seat Frame

Once back in the shop, start construction by cutting the seat rails and stringers from the 2x4s. As you probably know, dimensional lumber comes with rounded edges. You'll need to get rid of them. Cut the pieces for the rails and stringers to their 3" thickness by first running one edge over the jointer until

they have a square edge, then rip them to 3" wide. To give the seat a comfortable back angle, set your saw blade to a 7-degree bevel and run the back rail on edge to give a 7-degree angle to the back.

Now cut the pieces to length and screw the stringers between the rails, spacing them as shown. The center section spacing is critical because the pop-up table needs to be square so it can be lifted out and turned in place and the legs lowered. Use 2" galvanized deck screws when screwing the seat frame together.

Mill all the slats at the same time because they are essentially the same size. Cut the 1x4s into 24" lengths, and plane the boards to 5/8" thickness. Then rip them to their 2½" width and crosscut the seat slats to 20". To give the swing a finished look, cut an 1/8" roundover on all four top edges of each seat slat using a bit mounted in a router table. Attach the slats for the permanent seats, running the slats from side to side. They should flush up in length to the outside edges of the stringers, and the front slat should be flush to the front rail. Use about 3/8" spacing between the slats. I decided to attach the slats to the frame using finish

nails and an air nailer. This left a much smaller hole than screws, and it was very quick.

To finish the seat I decided to build the top surface of the table at this point. The spacing works the same as on the side seats, but run the slats from front to back. The slats are attached to two table battens (¾" x 1½" x 19⅞") that are held 1/16" or so away from the inside face of the front and rear rails. This gap should allow the table to lift out without binding, but some slight fitting may be necessary. Don't worry about the legs yet, we'll do that later.

Build the Back

Next, turn to the back of the swing. Mill the bottom back rail and two stiles to size as described earlier to leave crisp edges. Run the bottom edge of the bottom back rail and both stiles through the saw at an 83-degree angle to match the bevel on the seat. Then take the 2x8 top rail and lay out the top arch of the swing by marking the center of the rail, then mark 2½" down from the top at the center. Tap a small brad nail into the board at this spot, then put two more brad nails into the board at the bottom corner of the board at either end. Then take an eight-foot strip of ¼"-thick wood and bend it across the top nail, attaching the strip to the two lower nails with spring clamps. The arch formed by the strip can then be marked with a pencil, and then a second line marked 2½" above the first line. Jigsaw the piece to the outside of these lines, then sand the piece smooth.

To determine the length of the top rail, lay the bottom rail and side stiles flat with the bot-

Schedule of Materials: Garden Swing

NO.	LTR.	ITEM	DIMENSIONS (INCHES)			MATERIAL	COMMENTS
			T	W	L		
1	A	Bottom back rail	1½	5	55	Cedar	
2	B	Back stiles	1½	2½	20⅞	Cedar	
1	C	Top back rail	1½	8	60	Cedar	
11	D	Back slats	5/8	2½	20½	Cedar	Longest slat, cut to fit.
2	E	Seat rails	1½	3	60	Cedar	
4	F	Seat stringers	1½	3	17	Cedar	
21	G	Seat slats	5/8	2½	20	Cedar	
2	H	Arms	1¼	3	23½	Cedar	
2	I	Arm supports	1½	4	12	Cedar	Length oversize to allow fitting.
2	J	Table battens	¾	1½	19⅞	Cedar	
2	K	Table legs	1	1¼	6½	Cedar	
2	L	Table legs	1	1¼	8¼	Cedar	
2	M	Table leg braces	5/8	1¼	13	Cedar	Length oversize to allow fitting.
2	N	Table support cleats	1	2	20	Cedar	

With the seat frame assembled, nailing the slats in place was a cinch with a pneumatic finish nailer and stainless steel nails. Note the 7-degree bevel on the rear of the back seat rail.

tom rail between the stiles. Clamp these pieces in place, then lay the top rail across the tops of the stiles, flush to the top outside corner of each stile. With the top rail in place, mark the point where the inside curve of the rail intersects the inside edge of the stiles. Connect the two points and this is the angle to cut on the top edges of the stiles and on the ends of the top rail, to form mitered joints. The back frame will be held together with a double helping of biscuits, but first you need to cut the groove in the top and bottom rails to hold the slats.

Running the groove in the bottom

rail is fairly simple. Set up a router with a straight bit (or an up-spiral bit) of either ⅜" or ½" diameter. Next set up a fence on the router ⁷⁄₁₆" from the bit, and set the bit for a ½" depth. (The final depth is 1", but take it in two passes.) By running the router on both long edges of the rail, the groove will be centered on the piece. Check the fit of the back slats in the rail (or better, a test piece), then make the groove.

To cut the same groove in the arched top rail, see the photo at far left. You will need to adjust the depth of the final cut a bit to compensate for the curve of the arch. Miter the top rail to length, then check the fit of your slats in the grooves. The spacing between the slats should be about 2¼", but double-check your dimensions.

After cutting the double biscuits at the joints, place the slats in the bottom groove and locate the top rail in position on the slats. Mark the height and curve on each slat. Remove the slats, numbering them as you do. Now add 1" in length to the marks on the slats and cut them to their finished length using the band saw. You're now ready to glue up. I used polyurethane glue for all my glued joints. The polyurethane adhesive provides a strong water-resistant bond in even long-grain to short-grain Don't glue the slats in place, however. Place them in the grooves in their approximate positions, then after the frame has dried, use a brad nailer to tack the slats in place with a single brad at top and bottom, from

the back. To protect the lower rail from rot from standing water in the groove, cut blocks (called fillets) the size of the spaces and glue them in place.

You're now ready to glue and bolt the back to the seat. I used four ¼" threaded bolts with washers to bolt the bottom rail of the back to the back rail of the seat. Hold the bottom edges of each flush, and again use polyurethane glue on this joint.

Next cut the two arms and arm supports from 2x4 material and cut them to shape using the scaled drawings on the next page. You may want to cut the angle on the bottom of the support and on the back end of the arms, then fit them in place and confirm the location and angle of the top end of the supports. Attach the arms to the back with a long deck screw through the back stile. Glue the support to the arm and to the seat with ½" dowels between.

The last step is to put the legs on the table, and to notch and fit the support cleats. Start by cutting the leg pieces to the sizes given in the Schedule of Materials. They are two different lengths to allow the table to sit parallel to the ground, even though the swing itself is angled back. Round over the top end of each leg to allow it to swivel without catching, then drill ¼" clearance holes, ½" down and centered on the legs. Drill clearance holes in the table battens ½" up from the hottom edge, and 1" in from the inside corners. Attach the legs using ¼" x 2½" bolts with two washers on

Holding the arched top rail steady was the most difficult part of routing the top groove for the slats. Remember to make the cut in two passes on each side. In this photo you can see that the rail hasn't been cut for length yet, allowing extra support for the router at the beginning and end of the cut.

With the miters cut on the top rail and back stiles, space the slats and use the top rail to mark the angle and length of each slat, (adding 1").

The back of the arm is simply screwed in place through the back stile, while the support is attached to the arm and seat with dowels and polyurethane glue. Notice the foamy squeeze-out of the glue at the joints.

either side of the leg and a nylon-lined nut to hold the legs tight, but not immobile. Check the spacing between the legs (near the bolts) then cut the leg braces to fit, and screw them in place between the legs. Now head back to the saw and cut the two table support cleats to fit between the inside stringers. Clamp these in place, center the table in place left-to-right and mark the location of the legs. Remove the cleats and cut ⅞" x 1" notches on the leg locations. Then use a handsaw to trim the ends of the legs to form tongues to fit into the mortises you've just created in the cleats. Glue the cleats in place, and once dry, the table will drop into place in the cleats, holding the table steady. After adding ⅜" x 4" eye bolts to the front and rear of the swing seat, the swing is ready to hang.

With the notches cut in the support cleats, the two pieces can be glued in place in the seat frame.

Last, but not least, bolt the table legs in place to the table battens. Note the notches on the ends of the legs which drop into the previously cut notches to stabilize the table.

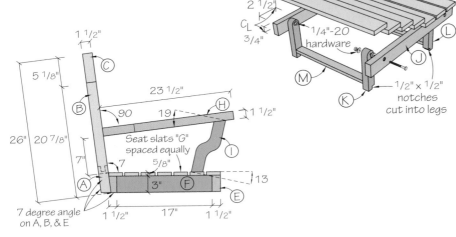

PROFILE

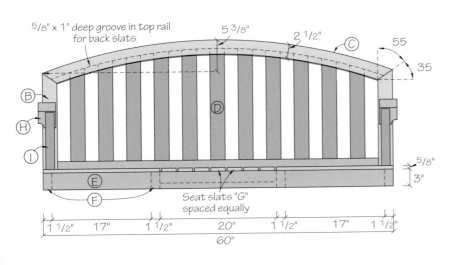

ELEVATION

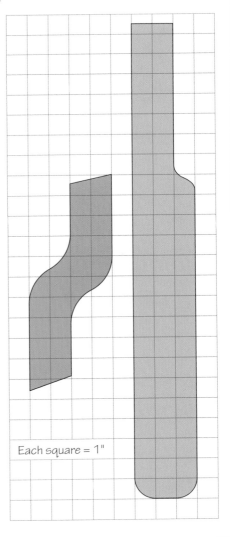

Each square = 1"

Norm Abram's Adirondack

BY STEVE SHANESY WITH NORM ABRAM

Editor Steve Shanesy builds an improved Adirondack chair with Norm Abram in The New Yankee Workshop. Build the chair and learn how Abram works.

I've become keenly aware throughout the years that patience allows time for opportunities to come along that might never have been possible. Such is the case with this Adirondack chair built in The New Yankee Workshop with Norm Abram.

Although projects similar to this one are rather common fare for most woodworking magazines, *Popular Woodworking* hasn't offered one to readers for more than 10 years. The project has been discussed, of course, but for one reason or another, it never happened. Then one day the phone rings and a representative of "The New Yankee Workshop" asks if we'd like to work with Abram to build the most popular project ever shown on the show.

Abram would build a chair and give it away as a promotion for the show and I'd build a duplicate as a project for the *Popular Woodworking* readers. Perfect!

OK, some of you are certainly wondering, "What is it like working with Abram right there in The New Yankee Workshop?" So let's get that part out of way. The most surprising thing was just how "Norm-al" it was, if you'll pardon the pun.

When you pare away all the myths and misinformation, Abram is just a very likeable, easy-going, hard-working, down-to-earth woodworker in a reasonably well-equipped, but not extravagantly so, woodshop. He was very much at home there. And it's not a TV studio set with woodworking equipment, but a real woodshop. How fancy? I've seen far more extravagant shops belonging to home woodworkers than this one.

Working with Abram was fun, to be sure. But I spent years working in commercial shops building hundreds of projects while working with others. And while Abram is a celebrity, his pleasant personality and easygoing manner made me feel right at home, too.

An Improved Adirondack Design

Now back to the project at hand: After getting acquainted at The New Yankee Workshop, Abram and I first inspected the original Adirondack he built, one based largely on a design his father had used years ago. It had weathered well and withstood the elements for more than a decade in continuous outdoor duty. He explained it was made from cypress, an excellent choice for outdoor projects, and he had laid in a supply for our new chairs.

We next reviewed the chair plans, one of those famous "measured drawr-ings"

Abram offers viewers at the conclusion of each show. This copy had some notes about minor modifications Abram intended as improvements. The last thing we did before cutting wood was review several templates he made for the original chair and saved throughout the years. We used these patterns for the curved parts. Drawings for these are included as part of the project plans presented here.

If you begin the project by preparing the patterns and stock to the rough sizes the building will move along pretty quickly. We completed our chairs in less than a day while working at a steady, but moderately easy, pace.

Starting at the Bottom

Essentially, this chair is built from the ground up so the first pieces required are the two side members that slope back from the front, vertical legs. Use the pattern to trace their shape on the stock, then cut them out using the band saw. Abram suggested we nail the two sides together at the ends in the waste material and stack cut them both to save some time. Then we drum-sanded the sawn edges to smooth the surface.

Next use a gauge block and a miter saw or table saw so you can repeat the

Norm Abram's Adirondack Chair

NO.	ITEM	DIMENSIONS (INCHES)			MATERIAL	COMMENTS
		T	W	L		
2	Side members	¾	5½	34¾	Cypress	
1	Lower rear crosspiece	¾	5½	22	Cypress	Use waste for rear seat slat
1	Front crosspiece	¾	3½	22	Cypress	
2	Front legs	¾	3½	23¼	Cypress	
2	Arm brackets	¾	3	6⅝	Cypress	
2	Arms	¾	5	27⁹⁄₁₆	Cypress	
1	Upper rear crosspiece	¾	4⁵⁄₁₆	26¼	Cypress	
1	Center back slat	¾	3½	30¾	Cypress	
2	Intermediate back slats	¾	3½	29⅝	Cypress	
2	Outer back slats	¾	3½	25¼	Cypress	
5	Seat slats	¾	2½	22	Cypress	

same length cut exactly for the lower rear crosspiece, the front crosspiece and the seat slats. Use the pattern that provides the curved shape of the lower rear crosspiece. (Abram's frugal, Yankee blood became evident when he pointed out that by using slightly wider stock than necessary for this part, the waste piece makes the perfect matched curve needed for the rear seat slat.) After band sawing, sand the edges smooth and be sure to set the waste piece aside for later use.

A Little Assembly Work

The first assembly chore is joining the two sides with the front and lower rear crosspieces. The crosspieces overlap the sides and care should be taken that the ends are flush to the outside edges of the sides. This will help keep your chair square as you build.

The chair parts are assembled using mostly screws, or in a few instances, carriage bolts, nuts and washers. We used stainless steel fasteners knowing they'd stand up to the rigors of life outdoors. These are more expensive than coated or plated fasteners, but in the end are a far better value. Screw lengths are 1⅝" except where noted. We also used outdoor adhesives. Abram used 3M brand Marine Adhesive Sealant 5200. Because my chair would be shipped to the *Popular Woodworking* shop in Ohio, I just screwed my parts together so it could be disassembled and more easily shipped. Later, back home, I re-assem-

Cut both chair side pieces at the same time by nailing them together in a waste section of wood. Band saw to the template line then sand the edges smooth.

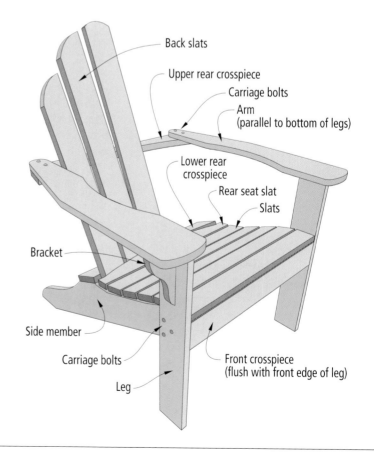

Back slats

Upper rear crosspiece

Carriage bolts

Arm
(parallel to bottom of legs)

Lower rear
crosspiece

Rear seat slat

Slats

Bracket

Side member

Carriage bolts

Leg

Front crosspiece
(flush with front edge of leg)

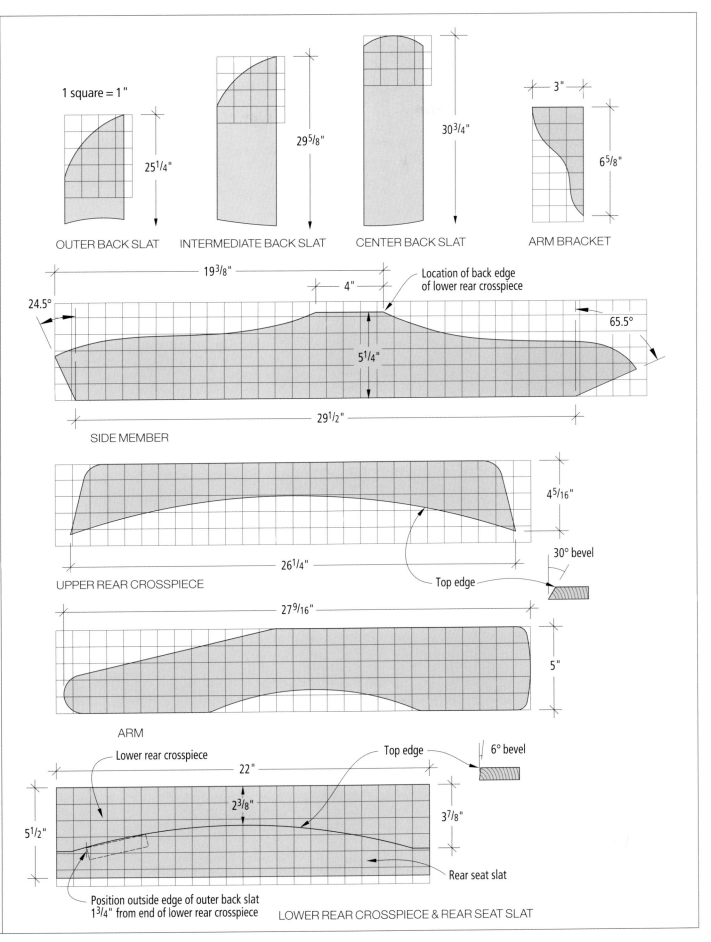

1 square = 1"

OUTER BACK SLAT — 25$\frac{1}{4}$"

INTERMEDIATE BACK SLAT — 29$\frac{5}{8}$"

CENTER BACK SLAT — 30$\frac{3}{4}$"

ARM BRACKET — 3", 6$\frac{5}{8}$"

SIDE MEMBER

19$\frac{3}{8}$" 4"

Location of back edge of lower rear crosspiece

24.5° 65.5°

5$\frac{1}{4}$"

29$\frac{1}{2}$"

UPPER REAR CROSSPIECE

4$\frac{5}{16}$"

26$\frac{1}{4}$"

30° bevel

Top edge

ARM

27$\frac{9}{16}$"

5"

LOWER REAR CROSSPIECE & REAR SEAT SLAT

Lower rear crosspiece

Top edge

6° bevel

22"

2$\frac{3}{8}$"

3$\frac{7}{8}$"

5$\frac{1}{2}$"

Rear seat slat

Position outside edge of outer back slat 1$\frac{3}{4}$" from end of lower rear crosspiece

Start the assembly by gluing and screwing the lower rear crosspiece to the chair sides. For lasting results, use a marine grade or waterproof glue, and stainless steel screws.

bled my chair using Titebond III because I couldn't find the product Abram used. In the Midwest, I guess we just don't have so much need for marine-grade adhesives as they do nearer the coasts.

All screw holes should be pre-drilled for a couple reasons; to prevent splitting by drilling a pilot hole and to countersink sufficiently to accept a wood plug later. The plug not only helps the appearance of the chair, but will also add to the chair's durability. We used a bit that drilled the hole and counterbored for the plug in the same operation.

Set up the two sides on the bench and first attach the lower rear crosspiece. When that's in place, turn the work over and fasten the front crosspiece. Use a pair of screws for each connection placing them about ¾" from the edges of the board.

Next the two front legs are attached using three, ¼" by 2"-long carriage bolts. Clamp the legs in position before drilling. The correct position is 11¾" from the bottom of the leg to the bottom of the front crosspiece.

When locating the bolt holes, arrange them in a triangle as shown in the diagram below. Following the diagram carefully prevented me from placing a hole where a screw for the front crosspiece might be located.

Attach the legs with the carriage bolts, heads to the outside. When tightening the nuts, prevent the head from turning by first seating the bolt head with a hammer blow, engaging the square corners underneath the head in the wood.

Drill ¼" holes through the side members and front leg to accept stainless steel carriage bolts. Use a clamp to hold the parts in position; the leg should be flush to the side's front edge and 11¾" up from the leg bottom to the bottom edge of the front crosspiece.

Arm and Arm Supports

The next parts to prepare and attach are the arms and arm brackets. Each requires use of a pattern and should be cut on the band saw. Sand the edges as before. Additionally, the top edges of the arms should be eased using a ⅜" roundover bit in a router. We routed only one edge, which designates it a top. So doing will create a right and left arm so choose your edges accordingly.

We attached the arm brackets first. The top, or wide part of the bracket, is positioned flush with the top of the leg and centered on the leg's width. Clamp each one in place then drill and countersink for the upper screw in each bracket. Repeat for the lower screw but use a shorter, 1¼" screw.

With the arm brackets in place, attach the arms to the front legs and bracket. Use the diagram at left to position the arm correctly before fastening. Again, be sure and use adhesive on each step of assembly as you proceed.

Building the Back

Now prepare the upper rear crosspiece. Prepare the part by using the pattern provided on page 41 for the inside curve. Note the inside cut is not only curved, but is cut at a 30° angle as well. Tilt the band saw table appropriately then saw the curve. Then return the band saw table to 0°, or square, and cut the ends. Sand the edges.

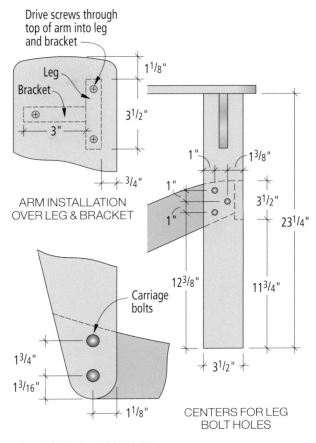

Drive screws through top of arm into leg and bracket

Leg Bracket

1⅛"

3½"

3"

¾"

ARM INSTALLATION OVER LEG & BRACKET

1"   1⅜"

1"

1"

1"

3½"

23¼"

12⅜"

11¾"

3½"

CENTERS FOR LEG BOLT HOLES

Carriage bolts

1¾"

1³⁄₁₆"

1⅛"

ARM INSTALLATION OVER REAR CROSSPIECE

Bolt the legs and side members together, bolt head to the outside with a nut and flat washer inside. Seat the square shank below the head with a hammer blow. The shank will prevent the bolt from turning in the hole.

Position and clamp the arm bracket then drill and countersink for two screws. The top edge of the support should be flush with the top of the leg and centered in the width dimension of the leg.

The upper rear crosspiece is attached below the chair arms. Use clamps to hold the piece in place as you position it correctly, that is, with a 20½" distance between the inside edges at the backs of the arms. That might leave up to a ¼" overhang of the arms at the outside edge. There should be sufficient space to secure the arms and crosspiece with two carriage bolts at each end. Use a spring clamp to hold the parts in place while drilling the ¼" holes for the bolts. When done, install the four bolts.

At this point, your Adirondack chair should begin to take shape. Aside from plugging the screw holes, only installation of the back and seat slats remain before the job is done.

Back Slats and Seat Slats

The back slats are the first slats to make. Prepare the back slats by using the patterns for the top edges as shown in the diagram on page 41, then band saw the shapes. Both back and seat slats should have their top edges rounded over using a ¼" roundover bit in a router mounted in a router table. Fan out the back pieces in their proper order to make sure you rout the correct edges.

Now install the back slats. To get the right look, proper spacing of the slats is important. Start with the center slat,

Use three screws to attach the arm to the leg and arm bracket. Carefully position the arm for a ¾" overhang of the leg. Use a spacer to help position it. The arm overhangs the front edge of the leg 1⅛".

placing it dead center in the back. I used four screws for each back slat, inserting one in the bottom, then made sure the top was positioned properly, then I secured it with three more. Be careful drilling the screw holes and countersink for the upper crosspiece as these must be done on an angle, drilling straight into the crosspiece, but at an angle to the back slat.

Next, install the outer back slats. Position the bottom of the slat 1" from the inside of the side piece. Secure it, then position the upper portion so that it touches the inside edge of the arm. Fasten it. Once both outside pieces are in place, the remaining two intermediate slats are merely positioned with equal spaces between their adjoining slats.

Now it's time to install the seat slats.

Start at the front with the front edge overhanging the front crosspiece by about ¼". Put one screw in each end and use two screws equally spaced attaching it to the front crosspiece.

Continue to add seat slats allowing ¼" spacing between them and fasten each slat with one screw at each end. The final seat slat is the one with the curve, which nests into the curve of the back. Leave space between this slat and the back so water can easily run off.

Finishing Touches

Before finishing up the chair, give in to the temptation to try it out! It's a surprisingly comfortable chair, definitely not the seat to offer a difficult mother-in-law.

Before a final sanding, I grabbed some fall-off cypress and cut about 60 plugs for filling the holes left from countersinking the screws. I used a narrow chisel to pop the plugs loose from the board. I glued the plugs in the holes, leaving them proud. A flexible, fine-tooth saw easily removed the excess plug material.

When all the plugs were glued in and trimmed, I gave my chair a good sanding (#150 grit). The relatively soft cypress sands easily. While sanding, I made sure any sharp edges were eased.

I decided to leave the cypress unfinished and allow the elements to eventually turn the light brown natural color to a silver gray. I figure by the time that happens, the color will complement what I expect my hair color to be in another 10 years.

Cut the upper rear crosspiece's inside curved edge at a 30° angle. Then return the band saw table to 0°, or square, and cut the round ends.

Hold the upper back crosspiece in place with clamps so that the arms are 20½" apart, then drill each side for two carriage bolts.

Start installing the back slats with the center slat first, then the outer slats. The last two intermediate slats are then easily positioned with equal spacing between their neighbors.

Jatoba Bench

BY BERT JOHANSEN

Ebony spacers and plugs add visual interest to this indoor-outdoor design.

My lovely wife asked me to build a bench for our entry hall. After considering the intended space—which consists of an 11' wall—I initially planned on an 8' bench and sketched several possible options. However, the more I considered the challenges of building such a long bench and crafting the joinery so that the bench wouldn't warp, I opted for two 4' benches instead. And although they are intended for indoor use, I decided to make them suitable for outside as well, because the final design is perfect for a garden bench and who knows what the grandkids will do when they inherit them?

Influenced by Japanese design and inspired by its versatility, I crafted this simple bench using hidden stainless steel hardware for durability in either indoor or outdoor settings. For materials I selected jatoba with ebony accents. Dimensions of the completed project are 48" x 19¼" x 14".

Procure the wood and hardware, then joint and surface-plane the stock to final thickness.

Lay out the parts and make the straight cuts on the table saw. Cut the legs and rails to final length, but leave the slats and stretcher an inch or two longer than the final dimension. It is a good idea to make an extra slat and an extra leg as you proceed, as tear-out when you machine the curved edges could be a problem.

Making the Bench Top
The top consists of nine slats and 16 ebony spacers, held together by two stainless-steel all-thread rods. Draw a fair curve for the top of the slats and create a template from ½" plywood. Sand the curved top edge smooth. (An oscillating spindle sander expedites this job—and many others in this project.) Drill ⁵⁄₁₆" holes exactly 10" from the ends of the template, as shown on the drawing

PATTERN-ROUT THE SLATS. Jatoba is very brittle and prone to splintering, so attention to grain direction while routing is essential to avoid tear-out.

START WITH A BLANK. A 6"-wide blank is ideal for laying out the slats so you can nest the parts.

MARK THE NOTCHES. Carefully mark the notches for the rails. Here, a lower rail blank is lying on top of the stretcher blank.

TIGHT IS KEY. Strive for a snug fit between the stretcher and lower rail.

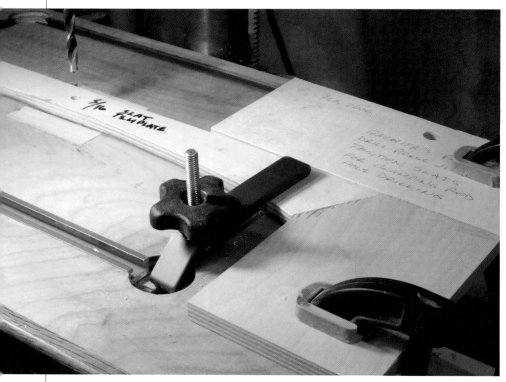

CRITICAL HOLES. Set up to drill ⁵⁄₁₆" holes in the slats. Both ends of the slats are secured with hold-downs for this critical operation.

LEVEL THE SLATS. I use my ancient (and very loud) belt sander to level the slats. This operation requires a light touch and good hearing protection.

on page 22. Use the template to trace the curved profile and cut the slats on your band saw, leaving about ¹⁄₁₆" outside the line. (Don't cut them to final length yet.)

Attach the template to each slat with double-stick tape and use a pattern-routing bit at the router table to clean up the band saw cuts. Be aware of the grain direction, as jatoba is brittle and can easily tear out during edge treatment. You may have to climb cut as you rout the rising edge.

Remove the template and cut the ends to final size using your miter saw set to 30°. Carefully sand the curved slats on the oscillating spindle sander, or with a sanding drum on your drill press. These surfaces are the most important aspect of the project, as they constitute the bench seat. Users will invariably caress the surface with their fingers, and you want to eliminate any "ripple" from the router bit—hence the importance of the sanding.

The center "keel" slat has an extra inch added to the bottom. As you will see, this allows the use of a bridle joint to attach the top to the top rails. As shown on the drawing, mark the notches, centered 10" from each end of the keel slat. At the same time, mark the notches for the lower stretcher, as the keel slat and stretcher must be aligned. Also mark the top and bottom rails for their notches. Raise your table saw blade to ½", make a test cut and adjust as necessary. Machine the notches in the keel slat and top rails. Sneak up on the final width, checking as you go for a snug fit. Reset the table saw blade height to 1⅜" and machine the two notch cuts in the stretcher, along with the notches in the bottom rails. Test-fit and clean up the notches with a shoulder plane or chisel.

With the notches completed, machine the curved edges of the keel slat and stretcher, repeating the process used for the slats—i.e. band saw, template-rout, cut to length and sand smooth.

Make a simple jig with a 30° notch as shown at left below. Use the slat template and jig to set up your drill press. Drill ⁵⁄₁₆" holes in the slats. Note that the two outside slats also receive ½"-deep counterbored holes, centered on the previously cut ⁵⁄₁₆" holes. Use a ⁵⁄₈" Forstner bit for these counterbored holes, and drill them while the slats are still in the clamps.

When all the slats are drilled, gang the slats together, secured with two ¼"-20 threaded rods (about 15" long) and corresponding ¼" washers and nuts. Number the slats for later re-assembly and sand them as a unit, first with a belt sander and finally with your random-orbit sander (ROS). Next, ease the edges with a ³⁄₁₆" roundover bit at the router table. As before, pay attention to grain direction. Finally, sand all slats individually with your ROS working up to #220 grit. (I find that Mirka's Abranet does a quick job on this tough wood.) There should be no sharp edges, except for the notches in the keel slat. I finished the process by hand-sanding with #600 grit.

Machine a piece of ebony to 1" x 1" x 12" and slice 16 ½"-spacers at the band saw. Each spacer receives a ⁵⁄₁₆" hole, centered by using a jig. This is a critical operation as the spacers must align perfectly during assembly. While at the band saw, cut four ³⁄₈"-long ebony plugs using a ⁵⁄₈" plug cutter. Also cut four jatoba plugs, which will be used later.

The top is now ready for assembly. Add washers and nuts to one end of the two threaded rods, with the nuts threaded just enough to be flush with the rod ends. Insert the rods through one of the outside slats so that the washer/nut combinations are recessed in the counterbored holes. Slide a spacer onto each rod, add a slat and repeat until all the slats are in place.

Add the washers and nuts to the other end of the threaded rods and snug the short end using a ⁷⁄₁₆" nut driver. (I discovered that not all ⁷⁄₁₆"-nut drivers will fit in the ⁵⁄₈" holes. I had success with a ¼"-drive set.) Measure the width of the top. You may find it somewhat different than the 13" dimension because slight differences in thickness of the slats or spacers are cumulative. In any case, the final width is important for cutting the threaded rod. Subtract ½" from the measured top width and record this number.

Disassemble the top and use a

PERFECT SLICES. After machining a piece of ebony to 1" x 1" x 12", slice 16½"-spacers at the band saw. And make a few extra, just in case.

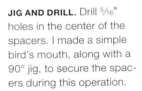

JIG AND DRILL. Drill ⁵⁄₁₆" holes in the center of the spacers. I made a simple bird's mouth, along with a 90° jig, to secure the spacers during this operation.

TOP ASSEMBLY. To start assembly, insert a rod through one of the outside slats so the washer and nuts are recessed in your counterbored holes. Slide on a spacer. Repeat.

hacksaw to cut the threaded rods to that length. File the ends of the rods to eliminate any sharp or jagged edges, and test them with the nuts to ensure they thread easily. Assemble the top as before and tighten the nuts "finger tight." Check and adjust the spacers so they are all aligned, then tighten the nuts firmly. Using a waterproof glue or epoxy, glue in the ebony plugs you made earlier. When cured, cut off the excess being careful not to mar the slats. Sand smooth to complete the top assembly.

1"

Keel slat

Upper rail

$^{13}/_{64}$" pilot hole

Mating line

$2^{1}/_{4}$"

1"

2"

$^{5}/_{8}$" counter bore

$^{5}/_{16}$" through hole

℄

BRIDLE JOINT MATING UPPER RAIL AND KEEL SLAT

60°

Notch for bridle joint with lower rail

$3^{1}/_{2}$"

$1^{3}/_{8}$"

$1^{1}/_{4}$"

$3^{1}/_{2}$"

STRETCHER DETAIL

$1^{1}/_{2}$"

1"

$1^{1}/_{2}$"

$^{1}/_{2}$"

$^{1}/_{2}$"

17"

$^{1}/_{2}$"

$^{1}/_{2}$"

$1^{1}/_{2}$"

$^{1}/_{2}$"

$2^{1}/_{4}$"

LEG DETAIL

$1^{1}/_{2}$"

1"

$1^{3}/_{8}$"

Notch for bridle joint with stretcher

$1^{3}/_{4}$"

$2^{3}/_{4}$"

$1^{1}/_{4}$"

$10^{1}/_{2}$"

14"

BOTTOM RAIL DETAIL

Notch for bridle joint with keel slat

1"

$^{1}/_{2}$"

$1^{3}/_{4}$"

$1^{1}/_{4}$" $2^{1}/_{4}$"

$10^{1}/_{2}$"

14"

TOP RAIL DETAIL

$2^{1}/_{4}$"

$3^{1}/_{4}$"

$1^{1}/_{8}$"

Notch for bridle joint with top rail

10"

$^{1}/_{2}$"

KEEL SLAT DETAIL

Jatoba Bench

NO.	ITEM	DIMENSIONS (INCHES)			MATERIAL
		T	W	L	
8	Regular slats	1	2¼	48	Jatoba
1	Keel slat	1	3¼	48	Jatoba
4	Legs	1½	2¼	17	Jatoba
1	Stretcher	1½	3½	35	Jatoba
2	Top rails	1⅛	2¼	14	Jatoba
2	Bottom rails	1¼	2¾	14	Jatoba
16	Spacers	½	1	1	Ebony
4	Plugs	⅝ dia.		¼	Ebony
4	Plugs	⅝ dia.		¼	Jatoba

HARDWARE					
2	Threaded rods	¼-20		12	Stainless steel
4	Nuts	¼			Stainless steel
4	Washers	¼			Stainless steel
2	Lag screws			2	Stainless steel
2	Lag screws			2½	Stainless steel

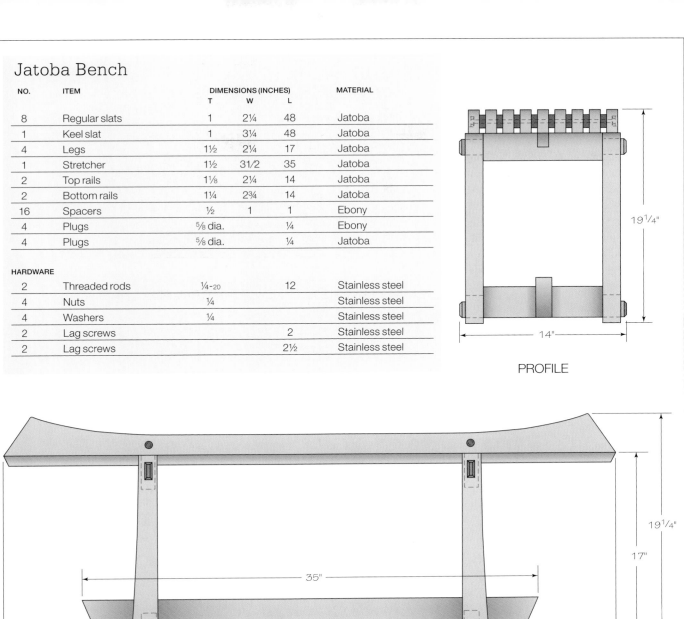

PROFILE

PLAN

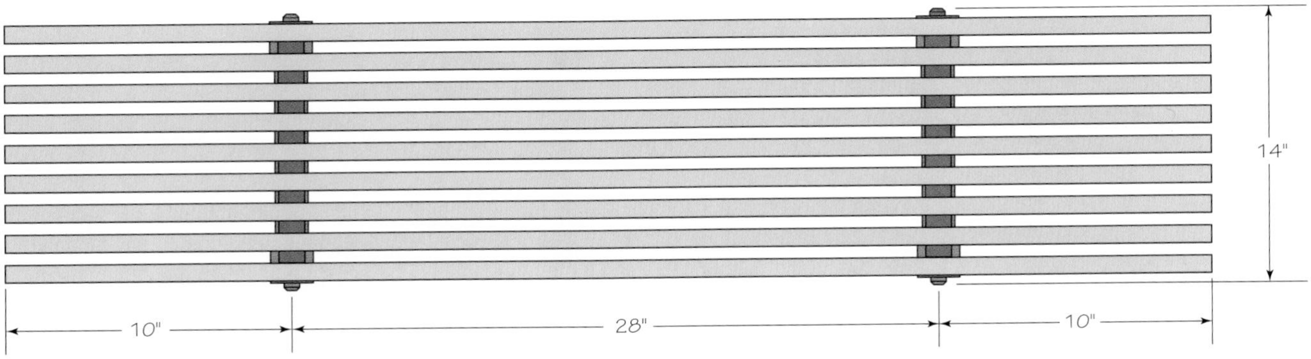

ELEVATION

Making the Legs

You previously machined leg blanks to 1½" x 2¼". As shown on the drawing (page 22), the legs taper from 1½" at the top to 2¼" at the bottom. Make a template of the fair curve, just as you did with the slats. Attach the template to the leg blanks with double-stick tape before machining them on the band saw. Because they are 1½" thick, instead of using a pattern bit on the router I used my oscillating spindle sander to bring them to final dimension. Ease the edges with a ³⁄₁₆" roundover bit. As with the slats, consider the grain orientation in this operation.

Mark the locations of the leg mortises and cut the mortises. I set up the horizontal slot mortiser on my Robland X-31 with a ½" spiral upcut bit. I milled all eight mortises and squared the corners with a sharp bench chisel.

Now for the rails. Note that the top and bottom rails are quite different. First, they have different thicknesses. I designed the bottom rails somewhat larger because the legs taper, and because the stretcher is robust. Also, note from the drawing that the tenons are located differently. The top rail must align with the top of the legs in order to form a flat surface and support the top. Thus the shoulder cut for the top rail tenon is ½" to match the topmost mortise cut. To give the mortises symmetry, the bottom mortise is placed ½" from the bottom of the leg. However, the rail should not extend to the floor. To solve this, I offset the tenon on the bottom rail, omit-

TIME-SAVING LAYOUT. Lay out the mortises on only one leg, which you'll use to set up the stops on your mortise—no need to mark the others.

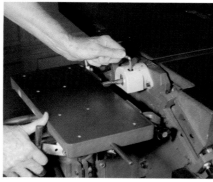

HORIZONAL MORTISES. I used the horiztontal mortiser with a ½" spiral-upcut bit on my Robland X-31 to machine the mortises in the legs

SETUP. Here, you can see where the plunge bit will enter the cut.

ALL SQUARE. Use a chisel to square your mortise corners as necessary.

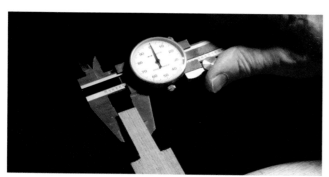

KEY MEASUREMENT. The fit of the milled tenons is critical to success, so check them with a dial caliper.

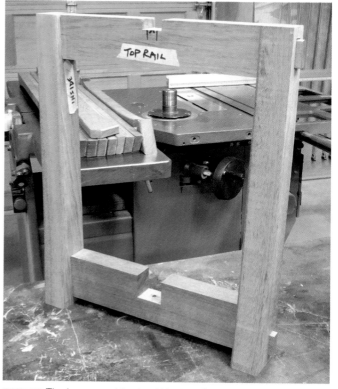

TEST FIT. The leg assembly should be test fit to make sure all the bridle joints are correct. Tweak as necessary before glue-up.

ting a shoulder cut in the process. Thus the lower rail begins ½" above the floor.

Machine ½"-thick tenons on both rails. I mounted a slot-cutting blade on the shaper and adjusted it to make the tenon cheek cuts. Make the shoulder cuts on the band saw and make final adjustments with a shoulder plane or bench chisel. "Dress" the ends of the through tenons with hand-cut chamfers. Next, drill ⅝"-counterbored holes ½" deep into the bottom of each rail, centered below the bridle-joint notches. Drill pilot holes for ¼" stainless steel lag screws to secure the top and stretcher. As with the slats, sand all pieces through #220-grit with your ROS, then finish by hand-sanding with #600 grit.

With all pieces machined, it is time for a trial assembly. Put together the leg assemblies and add the stretcher. Set the top in place. Check that all bridle joints are fully in place. Perform any last-minute tweaking as necessary. Glue and clamp the mortise-and-tenon joints on the legs and rails.

Finish and Final Assembly

Apply several coats of boiled linseed oil on all pieces, along with a top coat of wax. Complete the assembly by adding the lag screws to secure the bridle joints, then glue the jatoba plugs in the counterbored holes. Sand flush and finish with boiled linseed oil and wax. If you are planning to ship the bench to a client, omit the jatoba plugs and send the pieces flat. Add instructions and lag screws for the client to perform the final assembly.

CHAMFER. I finished the end of each through-tenon by clamping the workpiece into my bench vise, then clamped on a jig to hand-cut the chamfers.

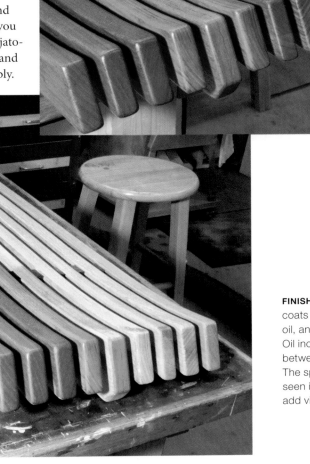

FINISH LINE. Apply several coats of boiled linseed oil, and a topcoat of wax. Oil increases the contrast between jatoba and ebony. The spacers and plugs, seen in the inset photos, add visual interest.

Dock Chair

BY SIMON WATTS

Lightweight, folding and portable, this chair is so simple to make you'll want a pair—or more.

I've always disliked the Adirondack chair and have never understood its popularity. I find it uncomfortable because the human frame does not bend at right angles and also, because it neither folds nor stacks, it's an awkward item to move and difficult to store.

When my daughter Rebecca showed me a wooden folding chair she had found in the attic of an old house in Nova Scotia, I was immediately struck by the ingenuity of the design, which combines comfort and convenience. Anyone familiar with Mies Van der Rohe's Barcelona chair will sense echoes of that famous and widely imitated design.

What I like to call my "dock chair" requires no special hardware and can be made with practically any wood, or combination of woods, in just a few hours. Anyone reasonably handy can make a pair of them in a weekend.

I made the first version using native pine and red oak slats fastened with bronze screws. I painted it signal yellow because the Nova Scotian fogs are notorious, and I didn't want to get run down by some errant vessel.

You'll see from the drawing at right that one frame fits inside the other with

a clearance of ⅛". This is so one frame can slide into the other for storage or moving, as demonstrated on page 29 by our colorful local boatbuilder Kevin Wambach.

I modified the original curves to make it lighter and more elegant and this version is shown in the drawing. I used Port Orford cedar for my newer version,

so the chair needs no finish and can be left out in the weather—rain or shine— and it will just turn an agreeable shade of grey. I didn't bother to make cushions for this chair but it would be no great matter to do so. I would use canvas— natural or synthetic—for the cover and stuff it with kapok. It would then double as a life raft if I fell off the dock.

Making the Dock Chair

About all you need for this project is a band saw (or jigsaw), a low-angle block plane, a drill and a spokeshave. For materials you won't do better than spruce for the frame because it combines light weight with flexible strength. Spruce does not weather well so the wood must be sealed with several coats of marine varnish or, for a really low-maintenance finish, paint. You could also make the chair in teak or mahogany. Either would weather well, but it would be much more expensive and less portable because of the additional weight.

The slats are screwed to the frame with stainless steel or bronze screws. Leave the heads exposed or plug the holes with wooden bungs.

Making Patterns

I've drawn the shapes of the crossed legs (see the illustrations on page 28) on a square grid. Each of the squares is 2". Rather than re-drawing, I recommend using a copying machine to enlarge the drawing.

You will have to tape several pieces of paper together to get the full-size image and may find some minor discontinuities—flat spots and abrupt changes in curvature. Rather than build these into your chair, take a flexible batten, spring it into the right shape and redraw the curves with a felt-tipped pen. This is often done by boat builders to generate fair curves.

Use these full-size templates to mark out the frames on your stock, nesting them if possible, and taking advantage of any natural curvature or "sweep" in the grain. If the stock is not wide enough, glue up two or more pieces until you have the width needed.

One of the clever features of this design is that the grain lines are almost

Supplies

Jamestown Distributors
800-497-0010 or
jamestowndistributors.com

oval-head bronze wood screws
#8 x 1¼, $22.58/ box of 100

Price correct at time of publication.

Dock Chair

NO.	ITEM	DIMENSIONS (INCHES) T	W	L	COMMENTS
2	Front leg frame	1¼	7⅜	40⅞	Shape to pattern
2	Rear leg frame	1¼	5⅞	33 ½	Shape to pattern
14	Slats	⅝	3	23½	Fit width and edges

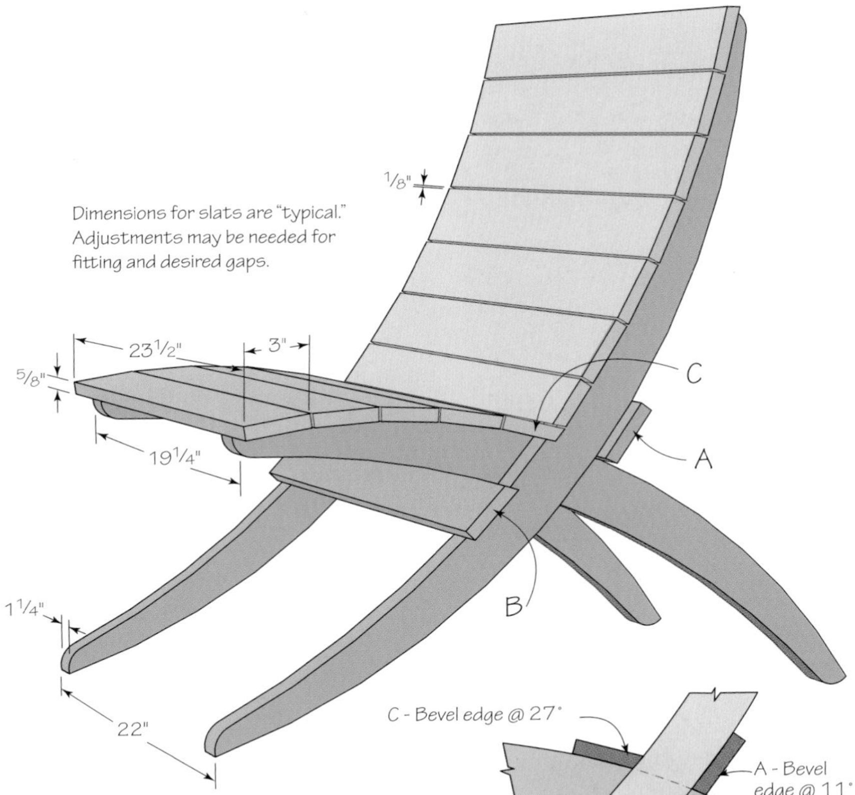

Dimensions for slats are "typical." Adjustments may be needed for fitting and desired gaps.
1/8"
23 1/2"
3"
5/8"
19 1/4"
1 1/4"
22"
C
A
B

DOCK CHAIR

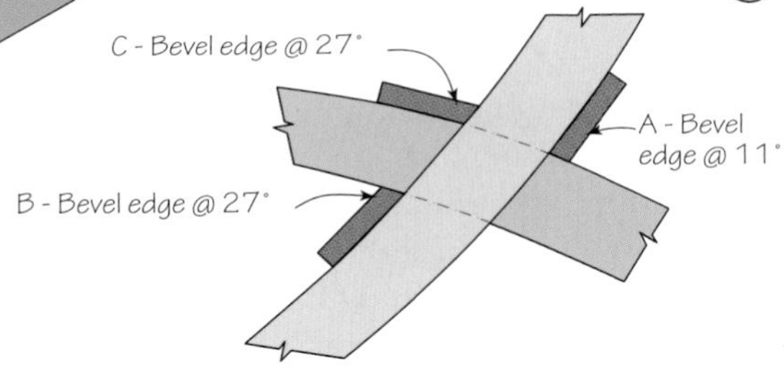

C - Bevel edge @ 27°
A - Bevel edge @ 11°
B - Bevel edge @ 27°

LOCKING SLATS DETAIL

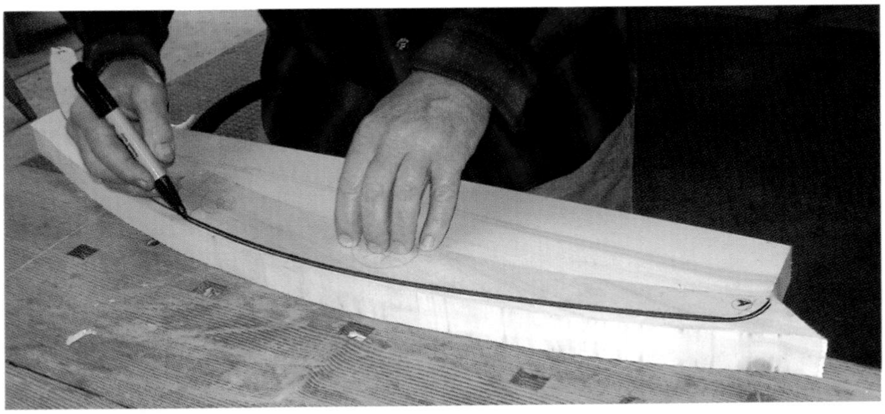

MARKING MULTIPLES. A template ensures that both frames match, and it speeds the process if you are making several chairs.

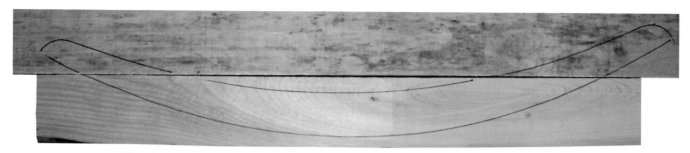

ADDING TO THE CURVE. To maintain straight grain at the intersection, you may have to add width to your frame stock.

straight at the point where the frames cross and the maximum bending stress occurs.

I have no band saw in my Nova Scotia workshop so I cut out each frame with a jigsaw then dressed the inside and outside curves with a spokeshave. This is a good time to do all the sanding and finishing, being sure to take the sharp edge off any corner with a sanding block. Give the frames a coat of primer (or varnish if using a clear finish), set them aside and cut out the seat and back slats.

If using a hardwood such as oak or ash, you can safely plane the slats down to ⅜". With softwood—pine or spruce—they should be at least ½" thick or even ⅝". The drawings and cut-list have them at ⅝".

Now use the template again to mark the exact position of each slat on both frames. Be precise in placing the locking slats, marked **A**, **B** and **C** in the drawing at left. These establish the angle one frame makes to the other and hence the comfort (or discomfort) of the completed chair.

It's well worth the extra trouble to plane a small flat on the convex side of the frame where a slat lands. You can also plane a very slight round on the inside of each slat before fastening it to the concave side of the frames. Otherwise you are likely to see unsightly gaps when looking at the chair from the side. Finish-sand the slats and seal them with paint or varnish as before.

The opening photo shows a hand hold so the frame can be easily carried. Include this feature if you wish—you can add one to the seat too if you wish.

Fitting and Fastening the Slats

If you plan to leave your chair out in the weather, leave at least a ¼" gap between slats so water can drain. Otherwise, ⅛" is sufficient. Make up some ¼" or ⅛" spacers to position the slats so the gaps are consistent for both seat and back, from top to bottom.

Start with material 3" wide for the slats. Depending on

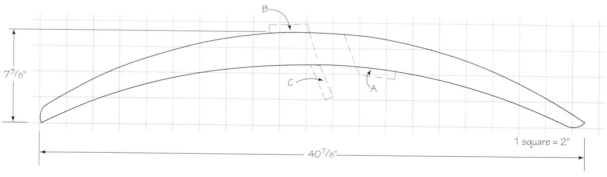

7³⁄₈"

40⁷⁄₈"

1 square = 2"

FRONT LEG PATTERN

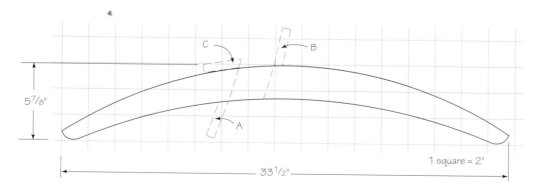

5⁷⁄₈"

33¹⁄₂"

1 square = 2"

REAR LEG PATTERN

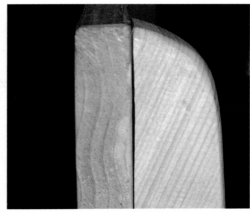

ALL IS FAIR. The spokeshave is ideal for removing saw marks and refining the curves. I find it easier to shape the outside before cutting the inside curve.

PLANE SPEAKING. Subtle angles and curves add detail to the chair. Work the long edges with a block plane, judging the angles by eye. When it looks good, it is the correct angle.

the gap between slats, and how much material you removed when shaping the frames, you may need to make individual slats slightly smaller. The top slat on the back is flush with the end of the frame.

Plane a bevel on the edge to meet the curved frame end at an attractive angle. Judge this angle by eye based on the drawing and photos. Some of the other slats may benefit from an angled edge to maintain a consistent gap between them.

Start at the top and fit and mark each slat before attaching any of them. The last slat above the seat will be about ½" narrower than the others. Start fitting the seat slats with the locking slat C in the drawing and work toward the end. The last slat can overhang the edge ¼" to ½", and the chair will be more comfortable if the edge is planed to a radius.

Fastening the Slats

Screwing is more durable than nailing, especially when using softwood frames, and is better able to bear the weight of a heavy person. Be sure to either countersink the screw heads (I use oval-headed bronze screws when I can get them) so they are a fraction below the surface, or counterbore and plug the holes.

Always set wooden bungs with paint or varnish, not glue, so they can be removed to refasten the chair if that ever becomes necessary. if you are pianning to use a clear finish be sure to put a drop of sealer (or marine bedding compound) in the pilot hole before driving the screw. Otherwise you are likely to get an unsightly ring around the fastener if the chair is left out in the weather.

Making the Cushions

You don't need a sail maker for this job but a local tent and awning maker will be able to handle lightweight canvas. I would simply have two rectangular cushions made, each one 16" x 24" and not more than 2" thick. They should have ties to secure them to the chair, or be connected with fabric hinges, so they don't blow away.

Instead of conventional sailcloth, I prefer a new product called Oceanus that looks and handles like canvas, and is available in solid colors. It won't mildew and resists degradation by sunlight.

I like this chair so much that I decided to make another version in aluminum with slats of teak. Holes drilled in the frames lightens the weight, and gives the frame the feel of an aircraft girder—in fact, I'm calling it the "flight deck chair."

SLIP FIT. The two curved frames slide together. When assembled as a seat, the three slats at the intersection keep it in position without any special hardware.

EASY TO STOW. The frames also slide together to allow for easy carrying and storage at the end of the season.

Adirondack Chair

BY CHRIS GLEASON

No book on outdoor woodworking would be complete if it left out the long-revered Adirondack chair. This classic piece of furniture is found in backyards and on porches all over the country.

Every time I build one, I feel like I'm paying homage to a great tradition that is well worth perpetuating. As I was writing this, curiosity got the best of me and I decided to do a little research into its history—I'm betting that you'll find it just as interesting as I did.

Excerpted from Wikipedia: The precursor to today's Adirondack chair was designed by Thomas Lee in 1903. He was on vacation in Westport, New York, in the heart of the Adirondack Mountains, and needed outdoor chairs for his summer home. He tested the first designs on his family. The original Adirondack chair was made with eleven pieces of wood, cut from a single board. It had a straight back and seat, which were set at

a slant to sit better on the steep mountain inclines of the area. It also featured wide armrests, which became a hallmark of the Adirondack chair.

The Westport chair may have never been documented if Mr. Lee had not offered his chair design to his hunting friend Harry Bunnell. The reason Mr. Lee did this was to help Harry make some money. Turns out Harry was broke and feared he would not make it through the winter. Trying to be helpful, Lee suggested he take his chair design and build it at his home carpentry shop to sell to the locals. As it turned out, Mr. Bunnell had more in mind, seeing Lee's chair design as a way he could make a future living. After doing some planning,

Bunnell took the chair design and filed for a patent on April 4, 1904. Later, on July 18, 1905, Bunnell received his patent for the chair he called the "Westport Chair". He never told his helpful friend Thomas Lee anything about applying for a patent, nor did Mr. Lee try to do anything later after he learned he received one. Bunnell became successful manufacturing and selling the chair for the next twenty-five years. He built all his Westport chairs with Hemlock or Basswood. He stamped his U.S. patent number on the backrest, painted them (a dark red-brown) or left them unpainted, and introduced several different variations (improvements you could say) over the years. His choice of Hemlock wood might seem odd because it is not a naturally durable wood nor is it considered a very suitable wood for furniture, but it was and is still readily available in the New England area. The chair never became wide spread as it never reached distribution further than a 100 square mile radius of Westport, New York. Even today, it still does not have the wide

Schedule of Materials: Adirondack Chair

LTR.	NO.	ITEM	STOCK	INCHES T	(MM) T	INCHES W	(MM) W	INCHES L	(MM) L
A	2	seat supports	2×6	1½	(38)	5½	(140)	37	(991)
B	2	front legs	2×4	1½	(38)	3½	(89)	25	(635)
C	5	seat slats	1×4	¾	(19)	3½	(89)	24	(610)
D	4	rear vertical slats	1×6	¾	(19)	5½	(140)	36	(914)
E	2	rear legs	1×4	¾	(19	3½	(89)	31	(787)
F	2	back support rails	1×4	¾	(19)	3½	(89)	21	(533)
G	2	arms	1×6	¾	(19)	5½	(140)	31	(787)
H	2	arm braces	1×2	¾	(19)	1½	(38)	7	(178)

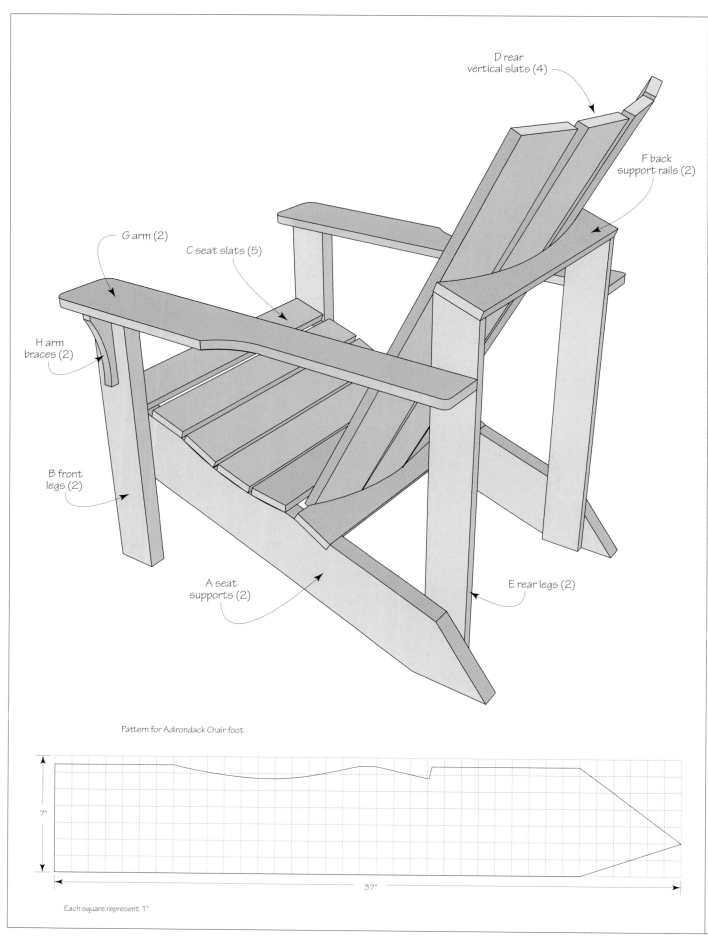

D rear
vertical slats (4)

F back
support rails (2)

G arm (2)

C seat slats (5)

H arm
braces (2)

B front
legs (2)

A seat
supports (2)

E rear legs (2)

Pattern for Adirondack Chair foot

7"

37"

Each square represent 1"

acceptance of the Adirondack chair, yet an original antique "Westport chair" that meets certain conditions can be valued at more than one thousand dollars.

Today, the Adirondack chair has evolved and can have any number of differences. Seats and backs with any number of slats, contoured or straight seats and backs, fancy curves here and there, built out of just about any wood you can think of. Different sizes and the number of legs round out today's variations, and I'm sure there are many I don't even know. However, there are still two main distinguishing hallmark characteristics of Bunnell's "Westport" chair made over 100 years ago. A true Adirondack chair has a raked, slanted back and the large broad armrests. Undoubtedly, the Adirondack chair has changed over the years, but for many it remains the truly all-American chair that has come to symbolize easy summertime living.

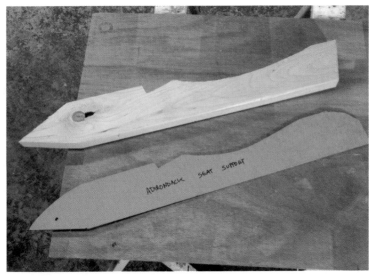

STEP ONE Building an Adirondack chair starts with the seat supports. I use 2×6 material here, as they need to beefy—most of the weight that the chair will hold ends up being transferred through these components. If you're only making one chair, you can simply cut out one support and then trace it to make the other one, but if you'll be building more than one chair, I suggest spending a few minutes to make a template of scrap ¼" plywood. I end up building at least one or two Adirondacks every summer, and it is pretty handy to just grab my template from where it hangs on the wall. In any event, I use a jigsaw to cut out the supports, although a band saw is a good choice as well. Feel free to incorporate any aesthetic modifications that you like, as indicated in the photo.

STEP TWO Once the supports have been cut out, the seat slats can be laid across them and secured with screws. Pre-drilling a clearance hole for the screws will prevent the ends of the slats from splitting.

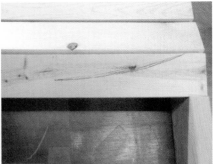

STEP THREE The back support rail is curved to help create the fan back that is a signature part of the Adirondack's look. My method for cutting this curve is a simple one—I begin by drawing half of the curve (from the outside edge to the midpoint). Leave about one-third of the rail's width intact at the bottom of the curve.

STEP FOUR Using a band saw or jigsaw, I cut along this line and remove the excess by cutting down the middle and then using this "waste" piece as a pattern for the other half of the cut. This ensures that the entire curve is at least symmetrical.

STEP FIVE Any irregularities can be smoothed out with a belt sander or drum sanders.

STEP SIX Although it is an unusual approach, I find that this approach is the fastest way for me to produce a pleasing curve on a one-off basis. This piece didn't take more than two or three minutes, and it will work just fine.

STEP SEVEN Since I was in the mode of cutting curves, I also cut out the back support rail for the top of the back. I used the same technique, but in this case the curve extends to the ends of the slat.

STEP EIGHT Here's a helpful view of the screws into the seat slats. I suggest placing the screws as far from the outside edge as possible to prevent splitting.

STEP NINE Once the lower part of the seat assembly is complete, the front legs can be attached. I left them longer than necessary at this point. I figured I could easily trim them down to a comfortable height when the time came. The legs should be bolted to the seat supports (flush to the front edge) with carriage bolts, but long screws will provide a fine temporary method of attachment.

STEP TEN The rear legs can be secured to the chair frame at this point. Hold the back edge of the leg flush to the top of the bevel at the rear of the seat support.

STEP 11 I screwed the upper back support rail to the tops of the rear legs, and this set the stage for me to begin laying out the fanned back slats.

STEP 12 Here's another view of the progress so far.

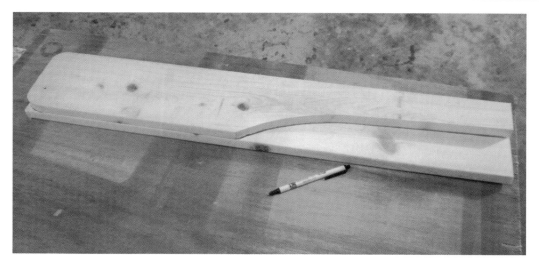

STEP 13 The sequence of events isn't too critical here—I jumped around a bit and decided to fabricate and attach the arms. In typical Adirondack fashion, they were fairly broad, and they feature a curve that tapers to a 2" width toward the back of the chair. Again, the shape can be personalized, so don't hesitate. Add radii to the front corners of the arms for comfort. Once I had cut out one, I used it as a pattern for the other arm.

STEP 14 By sitting in the chair and holding out my arms at a comfortable height, I was able to establish an ergonomically appealing height for the front legs. I cut them to this height and attached the arms and rear legs with screws.

STEP 15 Laying out the slats for the back takes a bit of experimentation. How many slats should you use? How wide should they be? How do you establish the spacing? Looking at the project from a few different angles helped me to answer these questions.

STEP 16 I ultimately decided to use four equal-sized slats for the back, and I spaced them such that they touched at the bottom and had equal gaps between them at their tops.

STEP 17 I decided to soften the look of the back by cutting a curve onto the tops of the two outermost slats. I sketched a line to represent this.

STEP 18 Once I cut out the curve on the top of the first slat, I used it as a pattern for the second.

STEP 19 Cutting the curves on the tops of the two slats made a big difference—the back looks just right to me now.

STEP 20 As both a practical and stylistic touch, I made a pair of small brackets (also known as corbels) to help support the broad arms of the Adirondack, which I was sure would loosen up a bit over time.

Garden Bench

BY CHRIS GLEASON

Here's a really versatile piece of furniture that would be at home in a variety of settings.

When I started looking around our yard, I found at least three places where I wanted one. The construction techniques are simple and low-tech: no table saw is required to make this bench, as it relies on dimensioned lumber (1×4s and 2×4s) straight from your local home center. You won't need a planer, either, because this kind of wood has already been surfaced at the mill. As far as tools go, you'll get by just fine with a drill, a jigsaw and a doweling jig. And long screws could be substituted for the dowels, too.

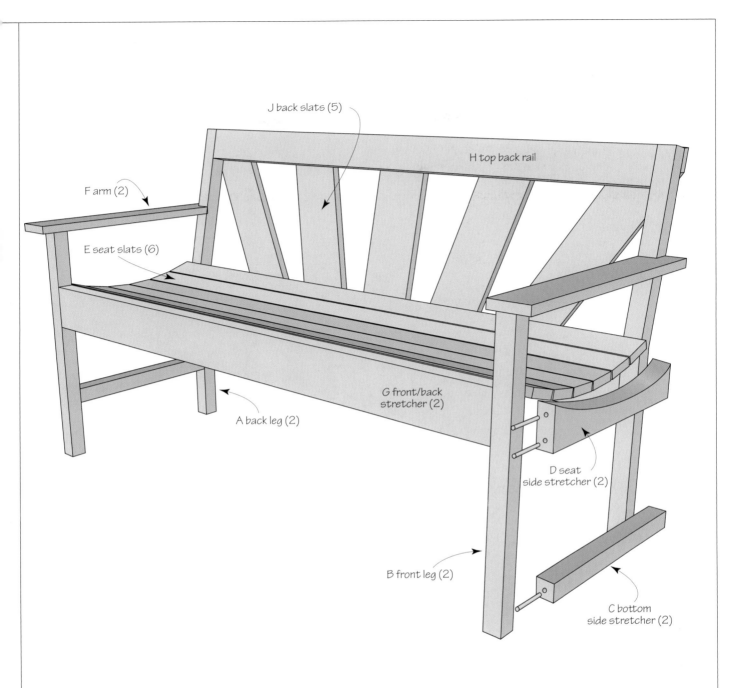

J back slats (5)

H top back rail

F arm (2)

E seat slats (6)

G front/back stretcher (2)

A back leg (2)

D seat side stretcher (2)

B front leg (2)

C bottom side stretcher (2)

Schedule of Materials: Garden Bench

LTR.	NO.	ITEM	STOCK	INCHES T	(MM) T	INCHES W	(MM) W	INCHES L	(MM) L	COMMENTS
A	2	back legs	2×4	1½	(38)	3½	(89)	34	(864)	cut to shape
B	2	front legs	2×2	1½	(38)	1½	(38)	24	(610)	
C	2	bottom side stretchers	2×2	1½	(38)	1½	(38)	16½	(419)	
D	3	seat side stretchers	2×4	1½	(38)	3½	(89)	16½	(419)	cut to shape
E	6	rear legs	1×4	¾	(19)	2⅝	(67)	54	(1372)	
F	2	back support rails	1×3	¾	(19)	3½	(89)	22	(559)	
G	2	arms	2×4	1½	(38)	3½	(89)	50	(1270)	
H	2	arm braces	2×4	1½	(38)	3½	(89)	50	(1270)	
J	5	back slats	1×6	¾	(19)	5½	(140)	24	(610)	trim to fit

I decided to paint the bench a bright blue color so that it would stand out and lend a funky touch to the garden that it would complement. Varying the finish would change the feel of the piece quite a bit, so I suggest staining it or painting it in whatever way best enhances your landscape.

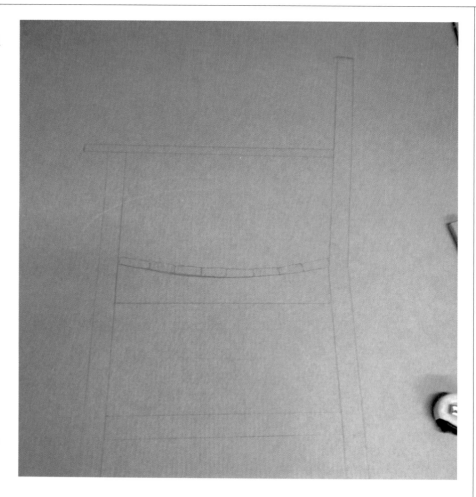

STEP ONE I find that the easiest way to begin a project like this is by building the sides first. To help me decide on the details of the design, I made a full-size drawing of the bench side.

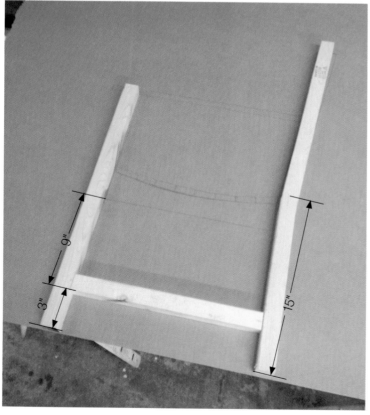

STEP TWO The drawing also comes in handy as a template for laying out the pieces and marking them for the joinery that will hold them together. I was able to determine that the lower stretcher should be placed 3" up from the bottom of the leg, and that the seat stretcher is located 12" up from the floor. The drawing also let me design the angle of the back leg, with the angle starting 15" from the floor. The back leg itself is cut to shape from a 2x4. I marked 15" up from one end along the left side for the "inside" of the leg. I then drew a line up to the top right corner of the 2x4, measuring over 1½" from the right edge. Voila, an angled leg.

STEP THREE I cut the two 2x4s for the seat side stretchers down from their 3½" width to 2¾" (to allow for the thickness of the seat slats). I then marked and cut a simple arc on the top edges, leaving 1¾" at the center of the arc. I decided to join the parts of the bench together with dowels, so the marks indicate a dowel location. They also serve as handy reference points that could help to quickly and easily reposition the pieces in the correct spots in case things get shuffled around, as they often do.

STEP FOUR This dowel jig is worth its weight in gold, and at $40 it is one of my favorite bang-for-your-buck tools. It automatically centers the hole across the width of the parts and accepts thick stock such as these legs and stretchers.

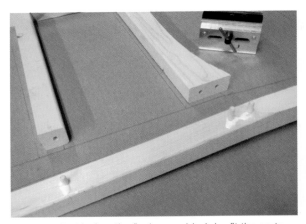

STEP FIVE Just before the final assembly, I dry-fit the parts to make sure they'll work. Then the joints go together with plenty of glue—more than you see in this photo—and make sure to apply adhesive to the entire dowel and the surrounding area.

STEP SIX Two clamps are sufficient to ensure good, even clamping pressure.

STEP SEVEN Two clamps are sufficient to ensure good, even clamping pressure. With the first side clamped up, the second goes together the same way—and it is usually a little bit quicker, as well, since you've just practiced it once. I like to lay the parts on top of the first side to double-check that the sides are identical and that no errors crept in the second time around.

STEP EIGHT Two clamps are sufficient to ensure good, even clamping pressure. Joining the sides with the seat boards helps the project really start to look good. I tack them in place with a brad nailer and then reinforce the joint with weather-resistant screws. Spacing the slats is easy since I'd already ripped them to the width indicated in the cutting list.

STEP NINE Two clamps are sufficient to ensure good, even clamping pressure. I put the front and back slats in first and then just set the middle ones in, maintaining small, even gaps between them all.

STEP TEN Two clamps are sufficient to ensure good, even clamping pressure. I used a 2×4 stretcher at the front of the bench to join the sides—this may be overkill, but it provides a lot of rigidity. I also added an identical one to the back of the bench.

STEP 11 The stretchers are positioned so that they're top edge is essentially flush with the seat slat closest to them. I secured the stretchers with long screws.

STEP 13 The arms could be shaped any way you like (taking a page from Adirondack chair design, perhaps), but I kept it simple here. They do need to be notched at the back edge so that they can fit around the rear leg.

STEP 12 Here's a nice picture of the overall progress.

STEP 14 I used a jig saw to cut the notch.

STEP 15 The arm can be attached to the front leg by simply screwing down through the top of the arm.

STEP 16 The back of the arm is easy to attach to the rear leg with a long, counter-bored screw.

STEP 17 To provide a safe and sturdy seat, I attached a brace on the underside of the slats. The profile matches the curve on the stretchers that hold the sides together.

STEP 18 The brace can be secured through the stretchers on the front and rear of the bench. I also recommend screwing and nailing down through the top of the slats into the brace.

STEP 19 I decided to make a fan-back for this bench as a way of breaking up its rectilinear nature just a bit. I think it added a rather playful touch. To lay out the back slats, I started with the easy part: the center slat simply runs perpendicular to the seat slats, and it is centered across the back. Once it was in place, I laid out the next two slats by eye—in this case, that meant that they needed to touch at the bottom of the fan and they were 6" apart when measured at the bottom of the top rail. I set them down with plenty of overhang on each end of the slats so that the excess could be trimmed away.

STEP 20 To determine how much extra material to remove, I drew a line along the bottom of the fan.

STEP 21 I also drew a line across the top. The top corner of the slat on the end needed to be trimmed to a point.

STEP 22 I didn't worry about the unevenness at the bottom of one of the slats because the back of the bench was going against a wall and so I decided not to sweat the small stuff.

STEP 23 The other side of the fan is laid out and trimmed in the same manner.

STEP 24 From the front, the effect is quite nice!

Porch Swing

BY CHRIS GLEASON

Usually a porch swing includes a back, seat and two arms or sides. With this clever design the back rolls into the seat and then continues on to create the arms!

I've seen a number of porch swing designs that look great at first but become a bit rickety over time. This is usually due to the joints that make up the frame of the swing loosening up. Given the forces exerted when one or two people swing back and forth, this is hardly surprising, and it almost starts to seem inevitable. I realized that the most vulnerable part of the swing is the portion of the frame that makes up the sides. It struck me that this problem could be solved in a number of ways, and one unique solution might entail constructing a frame that doesn't have joints at all. With no pivot points that could loos-en up over time, the whole structure would seem likely to hold up for much longer, as long as it was finished appropriately to handle the weather.

I initially considered building a side out of ¾" plywood, as it would certainly have enough stiffness, but I wanted to present a slightly more challenging solution. Since I'm always looking for ways to incorporate laminating techniques into my projects, this seemed like a neat way to do it.

If you've never laminated parts before, now's your chance. One of my main goals for this project—in addition to illustrat-

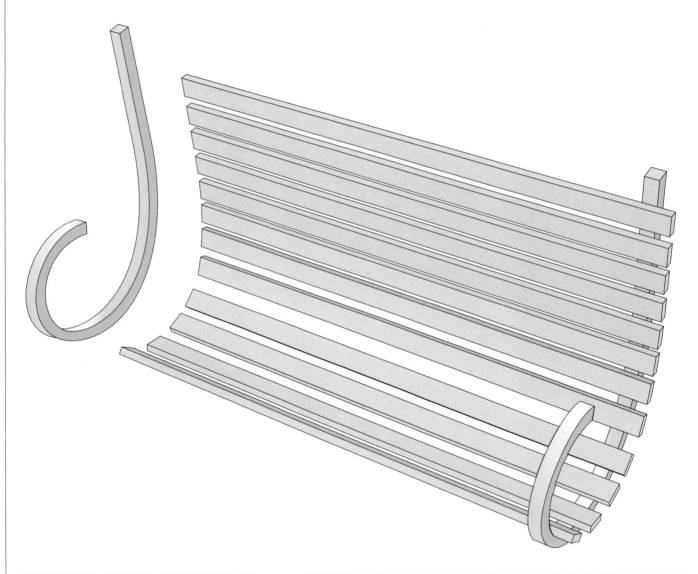

Schedule of Materials: Porch Swing

LTR.	NO.	ITEM	STOCK	INCHES T	(MM) T	INCHES W	(MM) W	INCHES L	(MM) L	COMMENTS
A	2	sides	pine	1½	(38)	1½	(38)	96	(2438)	after glueup, cut to length
B	12	seat/back slats	1×3	¾	(19)	2	(51)	48	(1219)	rip to width

ing how to build the swing, of course—is to present a comprehensive set of guidelines and tips for building bent laminations so that you can confidently add this useful technique to your repertoire of design strategies.

There are a few specialized techniques that people have traditionally used to create laminations. This includes methods such as steam bending, soaking the strips in water beforehand, or using a hot pipe. Some of these techniques are particularly useful when you want to bend thicker pieces of wood or you need to form a tighter radius, and while all of these techniques have their place, it was my goal to demonstrate that cold-bending thin strips around a moderately-sized radius is actually both simple, fast and effective.

STEP ONE To create the laminations for the sides of the bench, I needed 11 strips, slightly thinner than 1/8", per side to create a 1½" thick component. I cut almost thirty strips to get 22 usable ones, and the easiest way to do this is to set the fence in where you need it and then use a couple of standard accessories to safely cut the strips (safety items removed for this photo).

STEP TWO I suggest using a featherboard to keep the workpieces from wandering and producing non-standard strips.

STEP THREE A sacrificial push stick is also essential equipment. My shop has an unwritten rule that all push sticks must be shaped like animals, but this humor-intensive requirement isn't necessary.

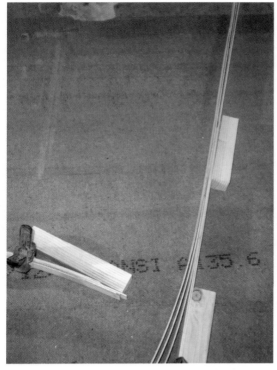

STEP FOUR The strips that I used for this lamination were 8', which was about 18" longer than I needed. I simply let the excess shoot out at the top. It will be trimmed later.

STEP FIVE The basic components required for building a laminated side for the porch swing are simple. A flat surface that is big enough to hold the side (4'×4' is more than adequate), a set of clamping blocks (scrap 2×2s or whatever is handy) and a drill and screws that will be used to fasten the blocks in place. Working from a full-sized drawing would be a good idea for a project like this, and I usually do, but in this case, the approximate shape and dimensions for the side were clear in my mind.

STEP SIX Working with a circular diameter of about 14", I just went for it and began laying out the required contour using one of my laminating strips and a few clamping blocks. The degree to which the strips will bend without breaking will depend on their thickness, the type of wood used, the presence (or absence) of knots, and how gingerly you work.

STEP SEVEN I secured the clamping blocks to the worksurface with screws that I drove in from the underside. I suggest working one curve at a time. As the blocks go into place, they can be used to hold the strip in position and then you can move onto the next spot that needs to be supported.

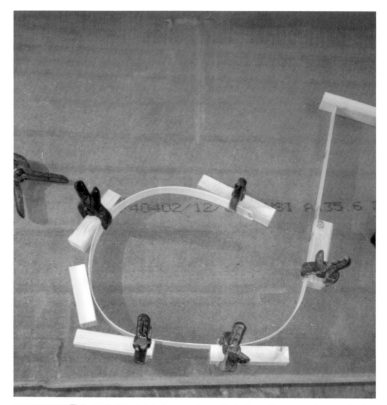

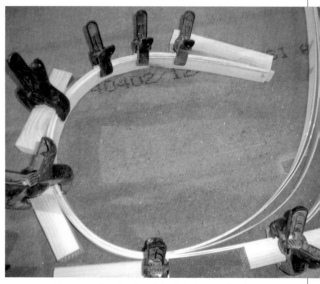

STEP EIGHT This technique results in a form that doesn't support every inch of the workpiece, but it provides excellent support on the key places in the lamination. This approach is fairly organic, and you have to pay close attention to how the strips are reacting as you lay out the blocks. You may find that in some places, you'll need to place a block right on the apogee of a curve, while other instances may require you to place blocks on either side of a curve.

STEP NINE Once you've finalized the blocks on the form, you can begin adding other strips so that they can start to bend themselves into the final shape. You'll pull them out later to apply the adhesive, but this step helps the strips start assuming their new shape and it will make the glue-up go more easily. It is also a critical way of testing the integrity of the strips—if any are going to crack (due to a knot or other problem), best to find out now.

STEP TEN When you're ready to glue up the first lamination, you can remove the strips from the form. Keping them in their exact order shouldn't matter. You can see how much the strips have already begun to conform to their new shape, even after only 15 or 20 minutes in the form.

STEP 11 Applying glue to the strips goes fairly quickly—I use a disposable foam brush to make sure that all surface are coated evenly. A certain amount of glue squeeze-out is inevitable. I find that small spring clamps like this are the most convenient way to hold everything in place. I think that every shop should have a bucket full of them—they're inexpensive and very useful.

STEP 12 Some of the clamps were used to anchor the lamination to the blocks, while others served to apply pressure to the lamination alone.

STEP 13 If the finished component sticks to the worksurface, a tap with a chisel and mallet should free it. If you really overdo the glue, you could have a problem with this, so setting down wax paper or the equivalent beneath the lamination wouldn't be a bad idea.

STEP 14 For my first lamination, I glued up eight strips—mostly because I was a bit nervous and was eager to see how it would come out. This required me to add three more strips and endure a second round of waiting for glue to dry, but this wasn't critical. In fact, breaking things down like this is a good strategy if you haven't done a lot of this kind of work in the past.

STEP 15 Because this sort of form doesn't support every bit of the lamination, there is room for variation each time it is used. I could readily imagine producing a set of parts which actually ended up being off by as much as 3/8"! To produce consistent results, I traced the contour of the lamination on the worksurface and used it as a guide to align the second set of strips. This common sense approach worked perfectly.

STEP 16 When I added the remaining three strips to complete the first lamination, I found that I could set the whole thing on the floor. This freed up the form for me to begin laying out the second side.

PRO TIP

You may find, once you have all of your blocks in place, that the contour of the lamination doesn't seem quite right. It may be too flat in some places or not curvy enough in others. It is a simple matter to just unscrew the required blocks and reposition them so that they push the strips into the desired shape.

STEP 17 Trimming the excess on both ends of the lamination could probably be accomplished in any number of ways. I used a hand saw because it was fast and easy.

STEP 19 I used a power planer instead—talk about quick and easy! Taking off about 1/32" per pass worked well.

STEP 18 People often recommend flattening the edges of the laminations on the jointer. This wasn't practical in this case because of the shape of the side, but it is an efficient method for simpler shapes.

STEP 21 To begin laying out the seat slats, I clamped the sides in an upright position. Even though the swing was laying on its back, it was the most definitive look yet at how the finished swing would shape up, and it helped me to see how to proceed.

STEP 20 A belt sander would be a reasonable alternative if you don't have a power planer. It works just as well and almost as quickly.

STEP 22 Beginning at the top of the seat, I began screwing slats to the sides, using an extra slat as a spacer.

STEP 23 Here you can see the swing sitting upright—finally!

STEP 24 I thought a cable might be a nice complement to the clean, modern design of this swing, but you could use chain or rope, too. Either way, a pair of eye hooks will need to be installed. Cable swages can be crimped using an inexpensive tool designed for the purpose. Just squeezing them in a vise is tempting, but it may not result in a strong and durable connection.

STEP 25 The cable attachment at the back of the swing was a little different—I inserted a hard plastic ferrule to ensure that the cable wouldn't abrade the surrounding wood.

STEP 26 A small metal hoop serves as a friction-free point of attachment for the cables that will connect the swing to the ceiling. I set the swing up in my shop first to see if it would work.

All-Weather Morris Chair

BY DAVID THIEL

An alternative to the ever-present Adirondack, the All-Weather Morris offers an adjustable back for comfort!

This project is special to me. It was the spark for all of my one-by furniture designs, and is still the most comfortable. The original All Weather Morris Chair was designed to fit a seat and back cushion. This made the chair comfortable, but if it had just rained and the cushions were wet, the bare chair wasn't designed for sitting comfortably. The chair shown here is version 4.0 and I've modified it to work with, or without cushions, and I've adjusted some design and building techniques. I think it's an excellent upgrade. Oh, did I mention the price? Built from pine, each chair runs about $60 in materials, plus the cost of the hinge. A good coat of exterior paint and you've got a great chair for under $100.

You might notice that the lumber in the photos looks a little weird. It is. Half of it is over 40 years old. In rehabbing our house, I pulled out some old pine closets. Rather than throw the boards away, I tucked them aside, and when this project came around, I knew I could be earth conscious and reuse them. Since the whole piece was getting painted, no one would be the wiser. I did cut all the pieces to standard home center sizes, so I wasn't cheating.

There are a lot of pieces to this chair, but if you go ahead and cut them all to length, assembly will move pretty quickly.

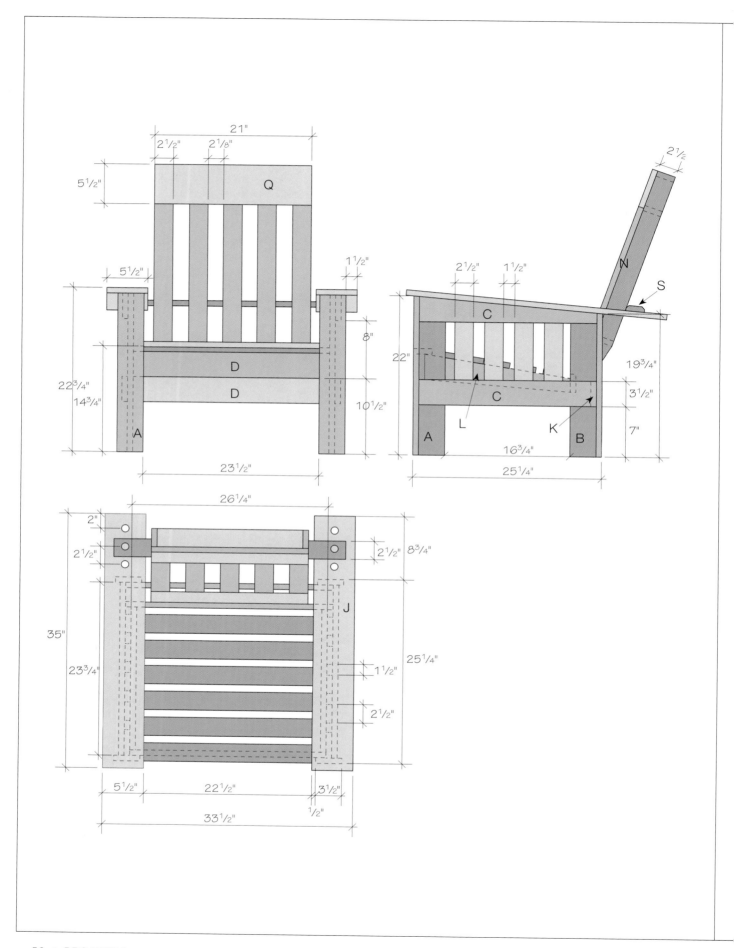

Schedule of Materials: All-Weather Morris Chair

LTR.	NO.	ITEM	STOCK	INCHES T	(MM) T	INCHES W	(MM) W	INCHES L	(MM) L	COMMENTS
A	4	front legs	pine	¾	(19)	3½	(89)	22	(559)	5° angle, one end
B	4	rear legs	pine	¾	(19)	3½	(89)	20	(508)	
C	4	side strtchrs	pine	¾	(19)	3½	(89)	23¾	(603)	5° slope on top edge of two
D	2	f&b stretchers	pine	¾	(19)	3½	(89)	26¼	(667)	
E	2	side slats	pine	¾	(19)	2½	(64)	14½	(368)	5° angle, one end
F	2	side slats	pine	¾	(19)	2½	(64)	14⅛	(359)	5° angle, one end
G	2	side slats	pine	¾	(19)	2½	(64)	13¾	(349)	5° angle, one end
H	2	side slats	pine	¾	(19)	2½	(64)	13½	(343)	5° angle, one end
J	2	arms	pine	¾	(19)	5½	(140)	35	(889)	
K	1	rear support	pine	¾	(19)	2½	(64)	26¼	(667)	
L	2	side spprts	pine	¾	(19)	5½	(140)	19½	(495)	Cut to match template.
M	6	seat slats	pine	¾	(19)	2½	(64)	26¼	(667)	
N	2	back frame	pine	¾	(19)	2½	(64)	30	(762)	
P	3	back frame	pine	¾	(19)	2½	(64)	19½	(495)	
Q	2	back plates	pine	¾	(19)	5½	(140)	21	(533)	
R	5	back slats	pine	¾	(19)	2½	(64)	19	(483)	
S	1	back suppport	pine	¾	(19)	2½	(64)	31	(787)	
T	2	dowels	hrdwd	1D	(25)			2	(51)	

STEP ONE The T-shaped front and back legs have a 5° bevel at the top. It's easiest to cut that bevel before assembly. With the four front- and rear-facing pieces cut to the length given in the cutting list, set the saw for a 5° bevel and trim one end of each piece.

Building the Legs

Each of the legs is made of two pieces of wood screwed together length-wise to create a T-shape. But to give the chairs their backward slope, the tops of the legs are cut back at a 5° angle. This means the front legs (with the flat piece facing forward) need a 5° angle on the top edge of the front piece, across the thickness of the board. The leg of the T that fits behind the front piece, needs a 5° cut from the front-to-back on the width of the board. This process is reversed on the two back legs, since the flat piece is to the rear of the leg. Take your time

marking and identifying the angles before making the cuts with your miter saw.

The chair is essentially screwed together. I used a countersink bit to drill clearance holes and recesses for wood plugs in one motion.

Start by marking the center of each flat piece of the front and back legs. Drill the countersink holes and screw the legs together.

STEP TWO Transfer the bevel location from the four cut pieces to the side-facing pieces of the legs. Remember that the front and rear legs are mirror images of one another, with the shorter "leg" pair to the rear. The legs are shown above positioned as they will be, with the rear (shorter) set on the left. The L's will become T's when the horizontal pieces are screwed to the center of the vertical pieces.

STEP THREE After marking the bevel locations, cut the other four pieces on the flat.

STEP FOUR All four legs have the leg of the T centered on the flat of the T. Mark the center line for screws.

STEP FIVE Drill three or four countersunk holes in each leg flat.

STEP SIX Then screw the leg pairs together, flushing the bevel ends to form the T. Pilot drill and countersink to avoid splitting.

STEP SEVEN The lower side stretchers are located up 7" from the bottom of each leg.

STEP EIGHT Screw the side stretchers in place on the outside of the legs.

STEP NINE Space the upper side stretcher 8" above the lower stretcher, which should be even at the top edge with the top edge of the front leg.

STEP TEN Connect your front and rear marks with a straight edge.

STEP 11 Jigsaw wide of your pencil mark to leave room for cleanup.

Making the Sides

To join the front and back legs to create left and right leg sets, mark up 7" on the outside of each leg. Make sure you have front and back pairs. Then screw the two lower side stretchers in place on the legs.

The upper side stretchers will require a 5° slope on the top edge. Place an upper stretcher in position, flush with the top edge of the front leg, and make sure the space between the stretchers is even at front and back. Then make a mark at the leg heights at both the front and back ends of the upper stretcher.

Connect the two marks to create a straight line, then cut the angle with a jigsaw. Clean up the cut with a bench plane if necessary. Mark the other upper stretcher the same way, then cut the slope.

Screw each upper stretcher in place on the outside of each leg, and you're getting closer.

To create the box of the chair, the front and back stretchers are screwed in place with the front stretcher located 10½" up on the inside of the front legs. The back stretcher is located 7" up on the inside of the back legs.

STEP 12 Screw the upper stretchers in place to complete the leg sides.

STEP 13 The front and back stretchers are screwed in place to the front and back legs. Check for squareness where the stretchers meet the legs.

STEP 14 I prefer to mark the slat lengths with each slat held in place.

STEP 15 A single screw in the center of each slat (top and bottom) holds things comfortably in place.

Side Slats

The next step is to attach the side slats. You'll see that I've provided individual lengths for each slat in the cutting list. Each slat also gets a 5° angle cut on the top edge. I've found it easiest to mark the locations of the slats (spaced 1⅜" apart, starting from the back of the front leg), then hold the slat in place and mark the angle on the top of each slat.

Because I want each slat top flush to the top of the upper side stretcher, I cut the slats a little short, letting the bottom of the slat fit up slightly from the bottom edge of the lower side stretchers.

Screw the slats in place with a single screw at top and bottom. I couldn't countersink these screws because the two ¾"-thick pieces don't allow enough room to add a plug. If you want to hide the

STEP 16 The seat supports fit flush to the top of the front stretcher, and attach to the slats.

STEP 17 At the rear of the seat support, a 1 x 3 is screwed in place between the two legs. Another screw from the rear holds the piece against the ends of the supports.

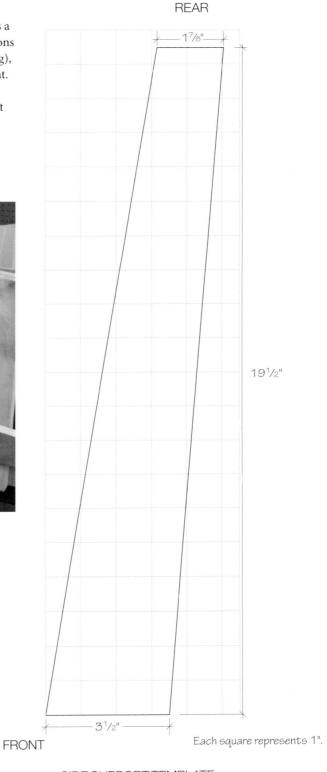

REAR

1⅞"

19½"

3½"

FRONT

Each square represents 1".

SIDE SUPPORT TEMPLATE

screws, then you will need to add wood putty and then sand it smooth. I just allowed the paint to hide the screw heads.

Side Supports

With the slats in place, I checked the pattern (shown on page 63) for the shape of each side seat support. Though the supports are cut from 1×6 boards, the only cuts necessary are on the two long edges. The short ends keep the "squared" cuts from cutting the 1×6's to length. Transfer the pattern to your board and cut the side supports to shape with your jigsaw.

Clean up the cut edges with a hand plane, then screw the supports in place on each side.

One last piece to hold things together. The rear support is the piece that will support the back frame of the chair. It's essentially a mount for the hinge. It's screwed between the two rear legs, and tight up against the back end of the two seat side supports. This piece is screwed through the back legs, and through the back support into the ends of the side supports.

More Slats and Arms

We're now ready to add the seat slats. This is pretty straightforward, with the slats spaced 1" apart. The front slat is notched ⅞"-deep to fit around the front legs, and then is screwed in place to the front stretcher. This allows an overhang on the front slat. The front slat gets four

STEP 18 After notching the front seat slat to fit around the legs, I used a roundover bit in my trim router to round the long edges of each slat. Less chance of pinching something important.

STEP 19 The front slat is screwed in place on the front stretcher.

STEP 20 The rest of the seat slats are screwed into the seat supports on either side.

screws, but all the others get two. A single screw on each end. I countersunk these holes for plugs.

The arms seem to bring things more than a step further somehow. One of the things that makes a Morris chair special is the ability to recline the back. To make this simple, three holes are drilled in the arms to offer three reclining positions. The holes are centered and at the back of each arm. The back support has two dowels attached that fit into the holes. This is also the reason why the arms extend so far beyond the back of the seat, and it's one of the things that makes this chair a Morris! Clever folks! The arms should overhang the legs 1" at the front and by 1½" on the outside edges.

STEP 21 The rest of the seat slats are screwed into the seat supports on either sideThe two arms are also rounded with the router, Then screwed in place.

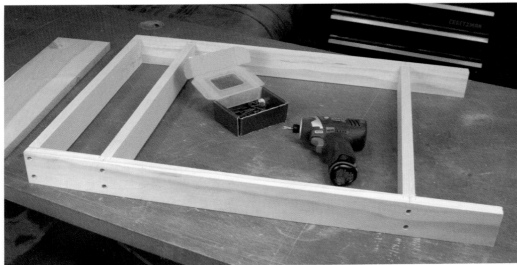

STEP 22 The rest of the seat slats are screwed into the seat supports on either side-Three cross members are screwed in place between the two frame sides.

STEP 23 The rest of the seat slats are screwed into the seat supports on either sideThe top and bottom plates are then screwed to the front of the frame, lipping only half way over the two middle cross members.

Building the Back

The chair back is screwed together (countersink for plugs) with three horizontal cross members. The two at the top are spaced to fit a headrest plate, and the bottom to accommodate a matching plate (for symmetry). Both the plates should cover only half of the horizontal cross member, allowing you to nail or screw both the plates and the back slats to the same cross member.

With the cross members positioned correctly, screw them in place through the back's frame sides. Next screw the top and bottom plates in place.

Lastly, to allow the proper swing of the back, clip the back corners of the seat at a 45° angle with your jigsaw.

To complete the back, simply screw the slats in place on the frame. The two outside slats are held flush to the sides of the back, with the other slats spaced evenly between. You'll notice a difference between the illustrations and the picture. On the chair in the front photo I used three 3½"-width slats, with two 2½" slats between. Either design is fine, I just decided to play a bit with the spacing. Feel free to be creative with your chair!

I rounded over the top edges of the back support (using my trim router), then drilled two ¼"-deep holes marked directly from the holes on the chair arms. By doing this rather than measuring, I'm assured a proper fit.

Next, the two 2"-long pieces of 1"-diameter dowels are screwed in place on the back support.

A good final sanding to all surfaces and I was ready to paint. Any decent Krylon color will put a great finish on the chair. I used spray cans, and honestly, it took about six, so prepare for that.

The last step is mount the back to the chair. I've used a variety of hinges over the years, but I've found I get the best look and performance from a continuous, or piano, hinge.

That's it! You're ready to kick back and enjoy the day.

STEP 24 The rest of the seat slats are screwed into the seat supports on either sideA 45-degree cut at the bottom of the back allows the back to swing to full-back position.

STEP 25 The rest of the seat slats are screwed into the seat supports on either side. The back slats are then screwed in place.

STEP 26 After carefully marking the location for the dowels on the back support, I drill a shallow hole to protect the top of the dowel from the weather, and to locate the dowel accurately.

STEP 27 The 2" chunk of dowel can then be glued (if you prefer) and/or screwed in place.

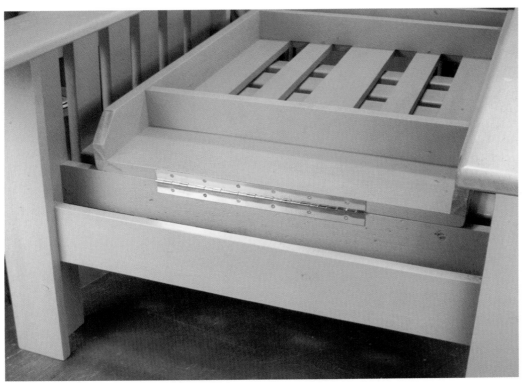

STEP 28 After painting, the last step is to screw the continuous hinge to the back, then rest it in place on the chair and screw the other leaf of the hinge in place on the back seat suppot.

Limbert Chair

BY DAVID THIEL

Painted outdoor projects add protection from the elements and add a splash of style to your project.

I love the outdoors. And I'm impressed with whatever forces in the universe have made it possible for me to purchase a collapsible canvas-and-metal camp chair for under $20. But when you're looking for furniture for a more permanent outdoor setting, then you need something special. This chair design caught my eye in a book called Arts & Crafts Furniture, by Kevin Rodel and Jonathan Binzen.

Actually there were two chairs similar in design. A nearly-black painted version by Scottish designer Charles Rennie Mackintosh that, it appears, influenced American designer Charles Limbert who created a wood-finished cafe chair. I liked the look of both chairs, and quickly recognized that they would easily adapt to our "minimal" approach to construction. My version here is an amalgam of the two, but because of my use of corbels under the arms, I'm going to give Charles Limbert the stronger claim. As my version was destined for use outside, I changed a lower shelf on the Limbert chair, to two stretchers at the front and back. This along with a seat made of slats, an angled seat and spacing for drainage all make this a more outdoor-friendly chair. I borrowed Mackintosh's painted finish, however, to help in weatherproofing the chair.

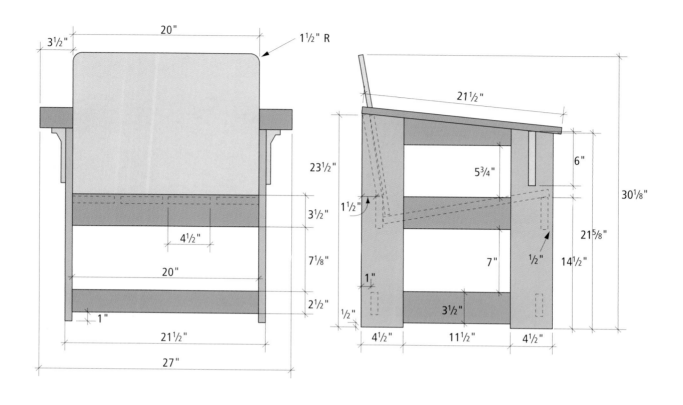

Schedule of Materials: Limbert Chair

LTR.	NO.	ITEM	STOCK	INCHES T	(MM) T	INCHES W	(MM) W	INCHES L	(MM) L	COMMENTS
A	2	front legs	poplar	¾	19	4½	115	22	559	Allows length for miter cut on one end.
B	2	back legs	poplar	¾	19	4½	115	24	610	Allows length for miter cut on one end.
C	6	side stretchers	poplar	¾	19	3½	89	11½	292	
D	2	f&b stretchers	poplar	¾	19	3½	89	20	508	
E	2	f&b stretchers	poplar	¾	19	2½	64	20	508	
F	2	arms	poplar	¾	19	3½	89	2½	546	
G	4	seat slats	poplar	¾	19	4½	115	18	457	
H	2	corbels	poplar	¾	19	1½	38	6	152	
J	1	back	plywd	⅝	16	20	508	18	457	
K	4	cleats	poplar	¾	19	¾	19	9	229	Cut to fit.

Ply and Poplar

My materials consisted of 1×3, 1×4 and 1×6 poplar boards, and a small piece of ⅝"-thick birch plywood. In drawing up the chair, I tried to use 5½"-wide boards for the legs and was disappointed with the final look. After some mental debate, I opted to rip the 1×6 boards for the legs to 4½" for a better look. If you're without a table saw, a jigsaw and a plane to clean up the edges will do in a pinch, but it definitely makes the project more time-intensive. You can also adapt the drawings here to accommodate the uncut 1×6 boards.

Start by cutting the side stretchers and legs to length (and width). Place the pieces on your work surface, and place them together spaced as shown in the diagram. Mark the height of the back leg at 23½" and the mark the height of the front leg at 21½". Then connect the points to define the angle at the top of the side leg assembly. We're marking this angle before the sides are assembled, because we need to make

STEP ONE The two sides are simple frames, though I did go the extra effort to make the vertical pieces thinner (4½"-wide) to provide more appealing proportions. Lay out the sides pieces to mark for pocket screws, making sure that you have both a left and right side.

STEP TWO My pocket screw jig makes quick work of the holes drilled in only the horizontal parts.

STEP THREE I used a parallel jaw clamp to hold each side frame tightly together as I inserted the screws.

STEP FOUR With both sides assembled, I double-checked my top lines for the arm slope.

STEP FIVE I used my jigsaw to cut each slope, staying slightly proud of the line, and then cleaned up the edge with my bench plane.

sure the pocket screws used to assemble the sides are located to provide the most strength. Be sure you make a left side and a right side. Otherwise you end up with pocket screws showing on the outside!

With the sides marked, I used my Kreg jig to drill pocket holes in the stretchers (two per end on the middle and lower stretchers, and on the top stretchers, two in the back and one in the front. Then I used a clamp to hold the side pieces tight and drove the screws into the legs. Again make sure you've got one left and one right side.

The Right Slant

I used a jigsaw to cut the top angle on each side. While this edge will be somewhat hidden by the arms, it's still best to make the cut slow and even for the best edge possible. You may want to touch up the edge with your bench plane.

Even though this was destined to be an outdoor project for me, I still opted to countersink the screw holes and add plugs. I knew it would give the chairs a more "finished" look. I located all the positions of the front and rear stretchers on the sides. Follow the diagrams to mark these locations, then drill the countersink holes for each stretcher in

STEP SIX The four stretchers are screwed in place through the sides. I used my countersinking pilot bit to make the clearance holes, anticipating plugging the holes afterward.

STEP SEVEN Holding the two sides together with the stretchers as you drive the screws home can be a bit of a juggle. A clamp or two, and using the other stretchers as spacers makes things more manageable.

STEP EIGHT I slipped the plywood back in place to test the fit, allowing the back to touch the top point of the side, and extend 7" above the sides.

the sides.

A clamp or two help hold things in place as you screw the stretchers between the two sides. It helps to use the other stretchers as spacers as you screw.

With your chair looking more cube-like, it's time to cut the plywood back to size using your circular saw. Then position the back between the sides with the height 7" above the seat back, and with the back resting against the back stretcher. Mark the location of the back on the sides, from the inside surfaces. Then remove the back and drill two clearance holes through the sides, stopping before the bit countersinks. Then work from the outside of the side assemblies and drill back through those holes, to countersink from the outside surface.

To finish the back, I marked 1½" radii at the top two corners. I then trimmed the corners to shape with my jigsaw.

STEP NINE The lower part of the back is braced against the back stretcher for more support. I then marked the location of the back on the inside surface of the sides.

STEP TEN With the back removed, I drilled two holes through each side, stopping with just the bit poking through the outside surface.

STEP 11 I then came from the outside surface of the sides, drilling deeper to countersink the holes for plugs.

STEP 12 With the back removed, I took the opportunity to mark each top corner with a 1¼"-radius and then used my jigsaw to make the cuts, rounding the corners.

Let's Try this Again

Here's where my planning failed. After screwing the back in place, I was using my daughter to test-sit the chair, and found that a reasonable amount of pressure against the back could force the plywood to split at the screw locations. I could have moved up to a ¾"-thick plywood back, but I liked the look and feel of the thinner ply, so I opted to add ¾" × ¾" bracing cleats behind the back, on both sides. I cut a long taper on each cleat to match the angle at the back. Then I counter-drilled the holes and screwed the cleats in place. More test-sitting proved that the fix was good, and not too ugly.

STEP 13 Next, I screwed the back in place and discovered a problem, The back wasn't thick enough to support the screw without the concern (as shown) of forcing the ply's apart when someone sits in the chair.

STEP 14 To add two braces behind the back I used a scrap piece of pine. I cut an angle on the braces so they wouldn't protrude beyond the sides. I used a Japanese dozuki saw to start the cut slowly.

STEP 15 After a moment or two, my scrap piece was cut in two.

STEP 16
I then marked both pieces for length, and made the cuts.

STEP 17 Some glue, a spring clamp and a couple of screws (in countersunk holes) added the braces and made the back much stronger.

I moved on to the seat slats next. These too I ended up ripping to 4½"-wide, though you could also use five 1×4s and adjust the spacing between the boards. As this is the place where the hide meets the pine, I added ¼" radius roundovers to the top edges of the seat slats. The slats were then attached using screws through the back stretcher at the back end, and finishing nails through the front edge and down into the front stretcher. Screws at the front of the slats are prone to scratching legs.

Arming the Chair

For the chair arms, I again added a roundover to the top edges, and then counter-drilled in four spots to attach the arm to the top of each side assembly.

Using the template on page 85, lay out the corbels and cut to shape with a jigsaw. If you have a band saw available, these pieces are an easier cut with the larger machine. I counter-drilled one hole from the inside to mount the corbels (a little glue here is a good idea), then added another screw to the corbel through the top of each arm.

STEP 18 I then cut the seat slats to length and used my router to round over two long and one short edge on the top of the slats.

STEP 19 The slats were then screwed in place through the back stretcher of the chair. I used another scrap piece to hold the side slats ¾" off the side frame, then evenly spaced the other two slats between them. I used an 18-gauge pneumatic pin nailer to attach the front of the slats to the front stretcher. You could also use countersunk screws, or brad nails for this step.

STEP 20 I next used my router to round over the top edges of the arms. I then pre-drilled and countersunk holes in the arms, and screwed them in place to the top of the sides. (Yes, that's Pete Townsend watching over my work.)

STEP 21 Use the template on page 78 to mark and cut out the arm support corbels. A jigsaw works, but if you've got a band saw handy, it's easier. Sand the corbels, and then add some glue and screw them in place through the inside surface of the side frames. I held my corbels about ¼" back from the front edge.

Finishing Touches

There are 50 holes in the chair, and I wanted them to disappear once the paint was on, so that meant 50, ⅜" wood plugs are glued in place, and then sanded flush (which took a little bit of time).

After the plugs are sanded flush, the whole chair needs a good sanding. Wherever two flat surfaces mate (such as the area shown in photo 20 at the right) this should be sanded as flush as possible. Assuming that you're using a solid color paint as I did, each of these mating edges will show up more dramatically than you might expect.

You should also spend a little time to take break all the edges of the chair to make it more comfortable to the touch. This is one of those steps that makes a huge difference. Sharp edges aren't worth rushing to the end of the project.

The last step is the paint. As you may have noticed in the opening photo, I built two of these chairs, and the first one was painted with a can of spray paint in a brown color. The spray paint didn't cover the surfaces as well as I prefered, and to be honest I wasn't too crazy about the color. So back to the store and I chose a quart of the red shown. It was worth the extra work.

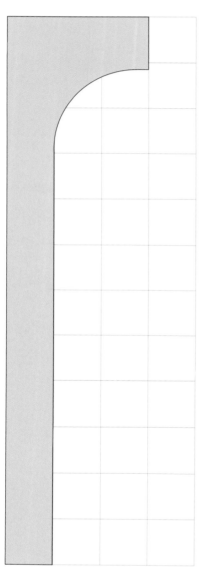

Each square = ½"

STEP 22 Now screw down through the arm and into the top of the corbel.

STEP 23 One of the longer steps is plugging all the screw holes and then sanding them flush. It's worth it to give the piece a finished look.

Garden Storage Bench

BY CHRISTOPHER SCHWARZ

Built to hold hoses, store garden tools and to last for years.

Outdoor Arts & Crafts furniture was almost always made from wicker or hickory sticks, so when it came to designing a garden bench in that style I had almost no examples to turn to. However, after collecting and building this type of furniture for almost a decade, I knew one thing had to be true: it would have to be built to last.

Fact is, I could have glued and screwed this whole thing together in a few hours. But because this bench was built for my sister-in-law as a gift for her new home (and because I don't want to be haunted by the ghost of Gustav Stickley), I decided to take the most traditional approach I could. That meant pegged mortise-and-tenon joints.

Schedule of Materials: Garden Storage Bench

NO.	ITEM	DIMENSIONS (INCHES)			MATERIAL	COMMENTS
		T	W	L		
2	Front legs	1½	1½	16	Redwood	
2	Back legs	1½	1½	34	Redwood	
4	Front/back pieces	1	7¼	45	Redwood	1" mitered tenon on both ends, included in measurement
4	Side pieces	1	7¼	18	Redwood	1" mitered tenon on both ends, included in measurement
1	Top rail	1	7¼	47¾	Redwood	2⅜" through-tenon on both ends, included in measurement
1	Bot. rail	1	4	47¾	Redwood	2⅜" through-tenon on both ends, included in measurement
1	Rear seat piece	1	6	48	Redwood	
1	Front seat piece	1	14	48	Redwood	
1	Seat support	1	3	16¾	Redwood	
2	Slat supports	1½	1½	42	Cedar	
8	Slats	¾	3	16¾	Cedar	

All Tenons, All the Time

Begin by cutting all your parts to size and laying out the ½"-thick x 2"-wide x 1"-long mortises on the four legs. Each 7¼"-wide slat in the lower case gets four tenons—that's two on each end. If I'd put only one wide tenon on each end, I would have had to remove too much material in the legs for the mortises. The detail drawing on the next page shows you how the mortises and tenons are spaced. Now cut your mortises. You'll notice that the mortises on the two adjacent sides meet in the middle of the leg. This means you'll have to miter your tenons on down the road.

Now lay out and cut the through-mortises on the back legs. The through-mortises for the top rail measure ½"-thick x 5¼"-wide. The through-mortises for the bottom rail measure ½"-thick x 2"-wide. Now cut your tenons and miter the ones for the lower case. To clean out the area between the two tenons on the lower case pieces, use a backsaw and a coping saw.

Cut the 2" arches on the front, sides and back pieces using a band saw. Clean up your work with sandpaper. Now locate where the center seat support will go and cut biscuit slots to hold it in place. Sand everything to 150 grit.

Assembly

After first dry-assembling your bench, glue up the bench in stages. First glue up the front pieces between the front legs and the back pieces between the back legs. I recommend polyure-thane glue here for two reasons. One, it's quite weather-resistant; and two, it has a long open time, which helps with this glue-up. Put glue in the mortises only, and be stingy. You don't want a lot of foamy squeeze-out. After the glue has cured, glue the side pieces and center seat support between the front and back leg assemblies.

Screw the two slat support pieces to the inside of the frame (one on the front, one on the back). Then screw the eight slats to the supports with about 2½" between each slat. Once that's done, peg all the mortises. I used ¼" x ¼" x 1¼" strips of walnut. First drill a ¼" hole that's 1⅛" deep. Carve the walnut strips round on one end, then hammer them home. Cut the waste flush.

Now work on the seat. Notch the rear seat piece around the legs. Attach it to the frame using cleats and screws. Then attach the front seat piece to the rear seat piece using the hand-forged hinges from Lee Valley. These are rustic, inexpensive but of excellent quality. You'll need to scare up some equally rustic screws to attach the hinges. I used some old #7 x 1" flathead screws.

Supplies

Lee Valley Tools
800-871-8158

3 Hand-forged hinges (1" x 6½")
item # 01A59.51 • $12.50 each

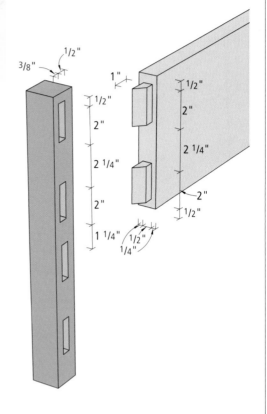

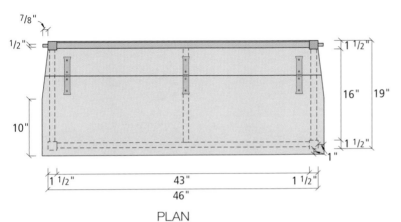

PLAN

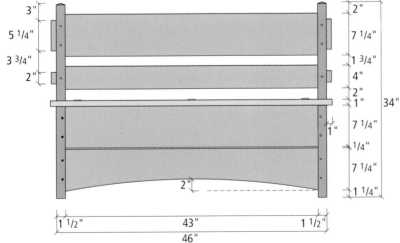

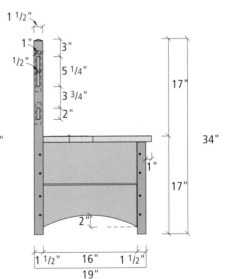

Titanic Deck Chair

BY DAVID THIEL

Only two deck chairs survived the sinking of the ill-fated oceanliner. Build your own reproduction with a band saw and a spindle sander.

Arranging deck chairs on the sinking *Titanic* is synonymous with futile gestures. Building a reproduction of one of the two known surviving chairs is anything but futile as you capture a piece of history and add an enduring piece of comfortable lounging furniture to the deck of your home.

Construction is more tedious than complicated, and two machines I found indispensible were a band saw and an oscillating edge belt/spindle sander from Ridgid. With all the interior and exterior curves, a spindle sander is almost essential, and Ridgid's combination machine made the job easier.

The first step is to plane the material to the proper thickness. I used 35 board feet of ⁸⁄₄ mahogany, though teak would be more true to the original. The mahogany cost $175 and hardware added another $45, which seems steep until you compare it to the $1,000 or more some stores charge for similar chairs.

Saw Twice

Start with the back crest rail and the arms. They're cut in a two-step process.

Use the patterns on pages 86 & 87 to mark the top and front surfaces of each piece. Cut the top or vertical pattern of the crest rail first, then lay the piece face up and cut the bottom of the pattern. Leave the top flat until you've cut the mortises in the rail. Allow the back surface to rest against the band saw's table, rocking the piece as you cut. On the arms, cut the top surface pattern first, then flip the piece onto the inside edge and make the second cut.

Shaped and Drilled

Use the templates in the PullOut Plans to lay out the rest of the pieces. Nest similar pieces (the back and foot rest slats, etc.) so you won't waste wood. Be sure to pay attention to grain direction on the legs. Maintain as much long-grain orientation as possible at stress points.

This is where the tedium begins. After band sawing each piece to rough size, sand it smooth. When cutting the slats for the seat and foot rest, leave the tenons uncut until the piece is sanded to shape, then mark the necessary ½"-thick tenon and cut it to finished size.

Next, mark the clearance holes and attachment points on the individual pieces, again using the patterns on pages 86 & 87.

Mortise and Fit

Now transfer the mortise locations from the templates to the crest and back lower rail, the seat sides and the foot rest sides. The foot rail mortises are straightforward, but the mortises on the seat sides need to

be cut free-hand, without using a fence. The mortises on the back crest need to be drilled at different depths as the piece is concave. Once the crest rail mortises are complete, band saw the top of the rail.

Assemble the chair before finishing to check the fit of all pieces. Start by assembling the back, center and front leg pieces with pivot hinges, and attach the arms to the center legs with drop-front hinges mounted to the bottom surface of the arm and the back edge of the leg. Make both the left and right sides, then attach the two halves by adding the stretchers and supports. The crest rail fits into beveled notches cut at the ends of each center leg. Use the rail itself to mark and fit the rail in place.

Next place the back slats in the mortises in the back lower rail, and clamp the rail in place between the front legs. The slats will extend over the front of the crest rail and must be marked and cut to fit into the ½"-deep mortises in the rail. With the slats cut to length, fit them into the crest rail mortises and screw the lower back rail in place.

With the exception of the seat and the foot rest, the chair is essentially assembled. You may note that the chair does not sit perfectly flat. Wait until the seat and foot rest are attached to trim the legs to adjust the stance.

For Sitting

The seat assembles with the slats flush to the top of the sides. The seat front and rear pieces are joined to the sides with dowels. Though the template should give you a good fit for the seat sides, check

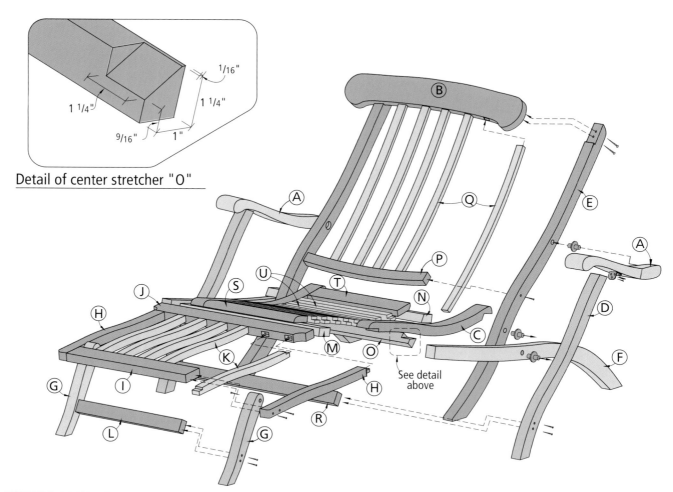

1/16"

1 1/4"

1 1/4"

9/16"

1"

Detail of center stretcher "O"

Schedule of Materials: Titanic Deck Chair

NO.	LTR.	ITEM	DIMENSIONS (INCHES)			COMMENTS
			T	W	L	
2	A	Arms	1¾	2½	18	Two-dimensional cuts
1	B	Crest rail	1¾	5	25¼	Two-dimensional cuts
2	C	Seat sides	1¾	2½	23½	Notched front & rear
2	D	Front legs	1¼	2½	24⅛	
2	E	Center legs	1¼	3	41¼	Notched for crest rail
2	F	Rear legs	1¼	5¾	37¾	
2	G	Footrest legs	1¼	1½	11½	
2	H	Footrest sides	1¼	1⅝	18	Drilled for threaded inserts
1	I	Footrest front	1	2½	17	
1	J	Footrest rear	1	2½	21¾	1"radius notches
5	K	Footrest slats	1	1¼	16½	Nest pieces to improve yield
1	L	Footrest stretcher	1	1⅜	14⁷⁄₁₆	
1	M	Seat support	1	2	20	Mortised for hinges
1	N	Seat support	1	2	22½	30° bevel on front edge
1	O	Center stretcher	1	1¼	22½	30° notch on ends
1	P	Back stretcher	1	2	17	
5	Q	Back slats	1	1⅜	22¾	Length is for longest slat
1	R	Front stretcher	⅞	1½	22⅞	
1	S	Seat front	¾	2½	13	Shaped front edge
1	T	Seat rear	¾	2½	13	Back cut at 30 degree bevel
8	U	Seat slats	¾	1	14	½ x ½" tenons included

HARDWARE DETAILS

Attach the footrest legs with threaded inserts and a brass screw.

Attach the footrest with sewing machine hinges mortised into the rails.

your pieces in place. With the seat fit, attach it to the chair frame with screws up through the seat support rails.

Details at the End of Your Journey

The footrest's sides are joined to the rear rail with tenons, and the front rail is screwed between the sides. Attach the sides before assembling the foot rest.

I recessed the hinges that attach the footrest into the surface of the front seat support and the rear foot rest rail using a trim router and straight bit. The chair is now complete. Adjust the stance of the chair by trimming the legs. Start by leveling the front and back legs. Once they are level, trim the center legs to match, and finally trim the foot rest legs.

Disassemble and mark all the pieces and sand them to 150 grit. To finish the chair I applied a mahogany stain and gave the entire piece a coat of exterior-grade urethane for protection.

Two details finish the piece. Before finishing, apply a stick-on five-pointed star in the center of the crest rail to mimic the carved logo of the White Star line on the original. You can add a brass card holder to the back of the crest rail which, on the original, was used to identify the passenger the deck chair was reserved for.

You're now ready to enjoy the turn-of-the-century luxury of a first-class deck chair. Feel free to arrange the chair as necessary.

Supplies

From Rockler
800-279-4441

3 pair - pivot hinges #51243, $12.99 per pair

2 pair - sewing machine hinges #32284, $17.99 per pair

1 - card holder #27946, (2 per package) - $6.69

2 - ¼-20 threaded brass inserts #33183 (8 per pack) $7.39

From Home Depot

Ridgid's Belt/Spindle Sander

2 - brass ¼-20 round head screws

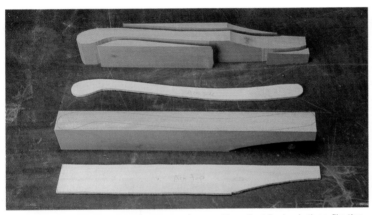

STEP ONE On the arms, cut the top surface pattern first (below), then flip the piece onto the inside edge and make the second cut (above). Be sure to make a left and right arm.

STEP TWO The pivot hinge hardware allows the chair to fold. But pay careful attention to left, right and inside and out when drilling the two-step holes.

LOWER STRETCHER

STEP THREE Using the lower stretcher to maintain the proper spacing, the crest rail is held in place and the notches are marked on the legs then cut and hand fit.

STEP FOUR With the mortises cut in the seat sides, assemble the seat and sand the surfaces flush and smooth. The seat remains loose and is screwed to the frame.

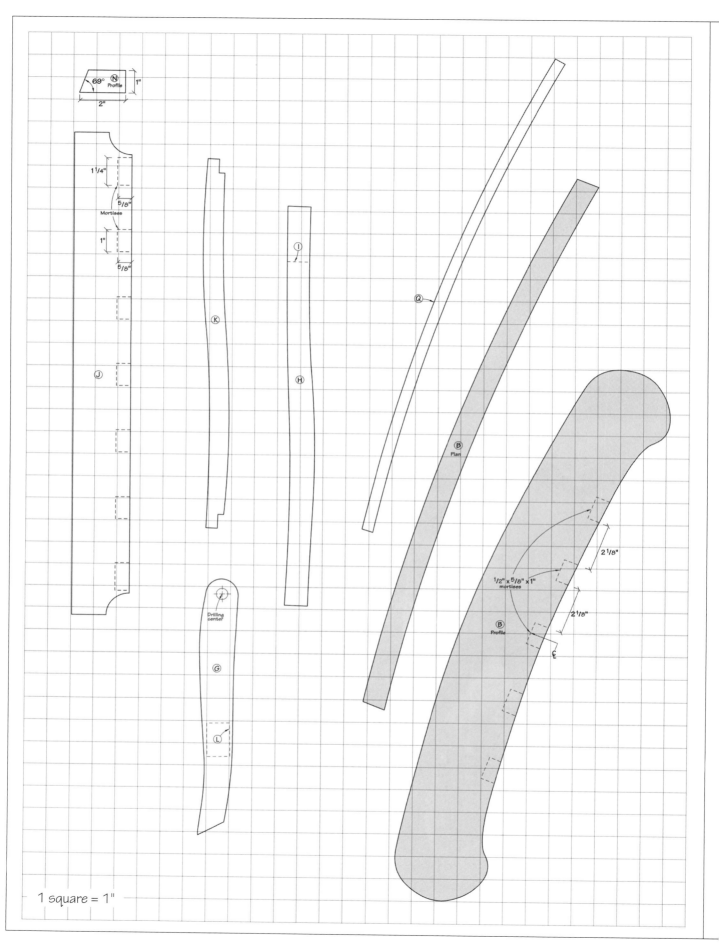

69°
Profile
Ⓝ
1"
2"

1 1/4"

5/8"
Mortise

1"

5/8"

Ⓙ

Ⓚ

Ⓘ

Ⓗ

Ⓠ

Ⓑ
Plan

Drilling
center

Ⓖ

Ⓛ

2 1/8"

1/2" x 5/8" x 1"
mortise

2 1/8"

Ⓑ
Profile

₵

1 square = 1"

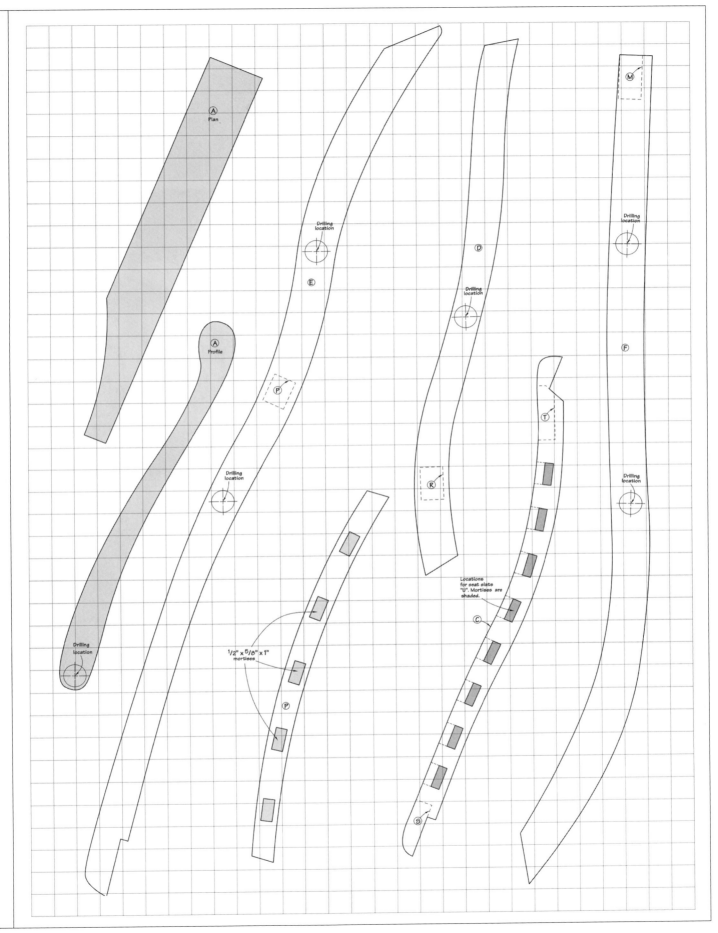

PROJECT 12

Chaise Lounge

BY DANNY PROULX

Required Tools

Table Saw or Circular Saw

Drill

Miter Box

Combination Square

Jigsaw

Hammer

Screw Gun or Drivers

Sander or Sandpaper and Block

Router Bits

Supplies

2½" Exterior-rated screws

2" Exterior-rated screws

1¼' Exterior-rated screws

1" Exterior-rated screws

Brad nails

Wood plugs

Polyurethane glue

Sikkens Cetol 1 #078 Natural finish

Bring the beach to your backyard with this classic lounge chair.

While on a recent vacation, we enjoyed the beach with many other vacationers who were reading and relaxing on chaise lounges. The lounges were comfortable, had an adjustable backrest, and were perfect for reading or a nap. But I had a problem finding a resting place for my drink and book. So I decided to build one of my own, complete with a pullout table.

This project is the result. It's built with construction-grade western red cedar. It's an ideal outdoor wood, but others, like redwood and cypress, would also be suitable. And the pullout tray is a feature you won't find on many models. The gently curved sides and adjustable headrest make this project well worth quality-control testing for an extended period of time.

This is another one of those projects that's reasonably priced. Check the cost on retail versions and you'll soon be convinced that this home-built chaise is well worth making.

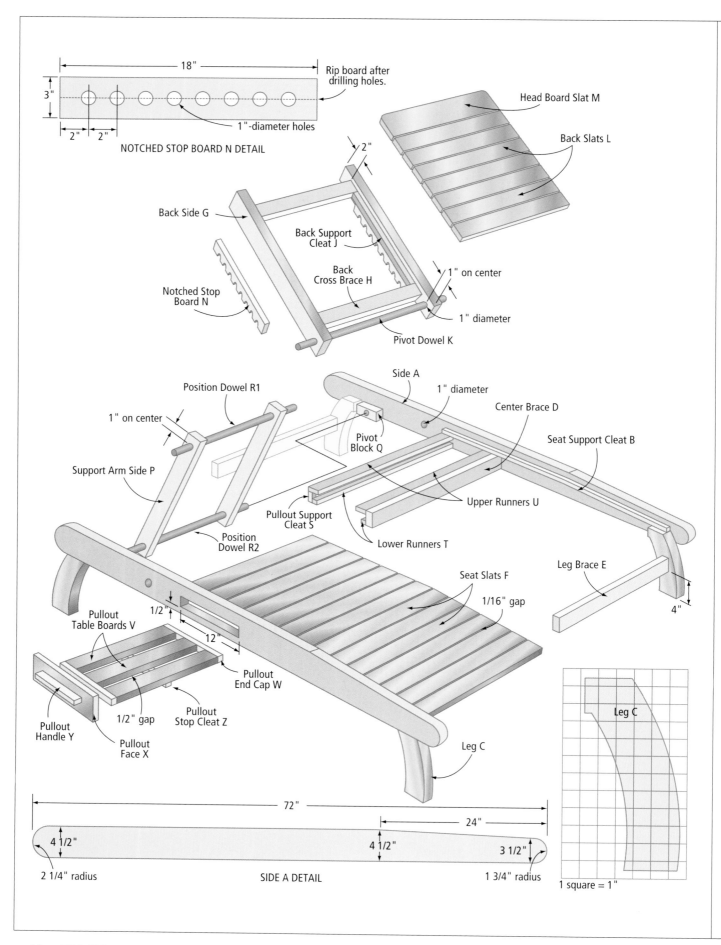

18"

3"

2" 2"

1"-diameter holes

Rip board after drilling holes.

NOTCHED STOP BOARD N DETAIL

Head Board Slat M

Back Slats L

2"

Back Side G

Back Support Cleat J

Back Cross Brace H

Notched Stop Board N

1" on center

1" diameter

Pivot Dowel K

Position Dowel R1

Side A

1" diameter

Center Brace D

1" on center

Pivot Block Q

Seat Support Cleat B

Support Arm Side P

Upper Runners U

Position Dowel R2

Pullout Support Cleat S

Lower Runners T

Leg Brace E

Seat Slats F

1/16" gap

4"

Pullout Table Boards V

1/2"

12"

Pullout End Cap W

Pullout Stop Cleat Z

1/2" gap

Pullout Face X

Pullout Handle Y

Leg C

72"

24"

4 1/2"

4 1/2"

3 1/2"

2 1/4" radius

SIDE A DETAIL

1 3/4" radius

Leg C

1 square = 1"

Schedule of Materials: Chaise Lounge

LTR.	NO.	ITEM	T	W	L	MATERIAL
			DIMENSIONS (INCHES)			
A	2	Sides	1½	4½	72	Cedar
B	2	Seat support cleats	¾	¾	48	Cedar
C	4	Leg blanks	1½	5½	11	Cedar
D	1	Center brace	1½	2½	23	Cedar
E	2	Leg braces	1½	2½	20	Cedar
F	14	Seat slats	¾	3½	23	Cedar
G	2	Back sides	1½	3	30	Cedar
H	2	Back cross braces	1½	2¼	19¾	Cedar
J	2	Back support cleats	¾	¾	22¾	Cedar
K	1	Pivot dowel	1 dia.		26	Cedar
L	7	Back slats	¾	3½	19¾	Cedar
M	1	Headboard slat	¾	5½	19¾	Cedar
N	1	Notched stop board	¾	3	18	Cedar
P	2	Support arm sides	1½	1½	12	Cedar
Q	2	Pivot blocks	1½	1½	4	Cedar
R	2	Position dowels	1 dia.		19½	Cedar
S	2	Pullout support cleats	¾	¾	2½	Cedar
T	2	Lower runners	¾	¾	23	Cedar
U	2	Upper runners	¾	1½	21½	Cedar
V	3	Pullout table boards	¾	3½	22	Cedar
W	2	Pullout end caps	¾	¾	11½	Cedar
X	1	Pullout face	¾	2½	14	Cedar
Y	1	Pullout handle	¾	1	9½	Cedar
Z	1	Pullout stop cleat	¾	1	9½	Cedar

TIP

Cut both sides from 1x6 lumber. Save the waste strips, as they can be used in step 2 as seat support cleats.

STEP ONE Prepare the two sides (A). Cut the radius ends and taper with a jigsaw or band saw. Then round over the edges and ends with a ⅜" roundover bit in a router.

STEP TWO Mark a line on the inside face of both side boards. This line is ¾" below the top edge of both boards and begins 2" from the foot end. Use a combination square and follow the curve with your line. Then as shown here, attach the two seat support cleats (B) to the sides. The cleats are thin enough to bend and follow the previously marked guide line. Begin the slats 2" from the foot end and attach with glue and 2" exterior-rated screws. These thin cleats can easily split, so drill pilot holes for the screws. Install the screws every 8" along the cleats.

STEP THREE Cut the four legs (C) from the leg blanks as detailed in the cutting list. Create a pattern so that all legs will be identical. Follow the diagram to form the pattern. It isn't critical that your legs match the drawing exactly, but try to draw them as close as possible. Cut the legs using a band saw or jigsaw. Before installing the legs, round over the two curves, as well as the bottom edges.

STEP FOUR Attach the legs to the side boards using glue and 2½" screws. The outside upper corner of each leg is installed 6" from the side ends. The top flat surface of each leg is 1½" down from the top edge of the side boards.

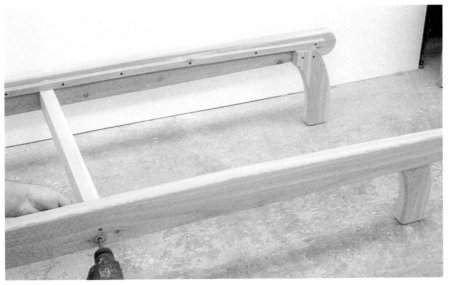

STEP FIVE Install the center brace (D) at the 36" mark on each side. The brace should be attached tightly under the seat support cleats (B). Use glue and two 2½" screws per joint, through the outside of the side board, and fill the counterbored holes with wood plugs.

STEP SIX The two leg braces (E) span the distance between each leg set. Cut them to length and round over all the edges with a ⅜" router bit. They are attached 4" up from the bottom of each leg, using glue and two 2½" screws per joint. Drill counterbored holes on the outside of each leg into the ends of the braces. Fill the holes with wood plugs. The leg braces should be centered on each inside leg face.

TIP

Cut 4" spacer blocks to help align the legs. It's easier to locate the braces accurately with blocks rather than trying to hold them in place.

STEP SEVEN Prepare the 14 seat slats (F) by cutting to length and rounding over each upper end on all the boards with a ⅜" roundover bit in a router. The first slat at the foot end also requires its outside edge rounded over. Install it so the outside edge is ½" past the seat support cleats. I butted my boards together because the wood I'm using has a high moisture content. It wasn't kiln dried, so I expect some shrinkage. If your wood is dry, space the boards ¹⁄₁₆" apart. Trim the last board so it stops flush with the end of the seat support cleats. Glue and screw the boards in place with 1" screws. Drill the pilot and counterbored holes so they can be filled with wood plugs.

STEP EIGHT Cut the two back sides (G). Sand and round over all the edges on both pieces. The two back cross braces (H) join the back sides. They are secured with glue and 2½" screws. As shown here, drill and counterbore screw holes through the outside face of each back side and drive the screws into each brace. Locate them 2" in from each end and flush with the bottom edge of the side boards.

STEP NINE The two back support cleats (J) run between the back cross braces (H). Attach them with glue and 2" screws, flush with the upper edge of the braces.

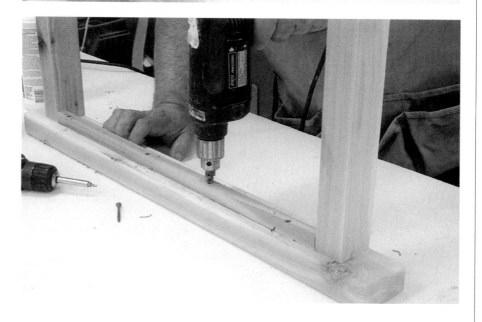

STEP TEN Drill a 1"-diameter hole through one end of each back side board (G). The hole is centered 1" from the end and in the middle of each face. Clamp the back assembly in place with ⅛" spacers on each side. Position it ½" away from the fixed seat slat so it can move freely. Then as shown here, use the previously drilled holes in the back assembly as a guide to locate and drill holes in the side boards (A). Remove the back assembly and drill a 1"-diameter hole through each side board.

STEP 11 Cut the 26"-long pivot dowel (K). Push it through the two sides and back assembly so it's flush with the two outside faces. Apply glue to the ends that are in the two side board holes only. Prepare the headboard slat (M) by cutting a small arc at each outside corner to remove the sharp edges. Round over the ends of all the back slats (L), as well as the outside edges of the bottom and head boards. Then as shown here, use glue and 1¼" screws in counter-bored holes to install the back slats. Install the bottom back slat first, aligned flush with the ends of the back side boards. Fill the counterbored holes with wood plugs.

STEP 12 Begin building the adjustable back mechanism by cutting a notched stop board (N). Drill a series of eight 1"-diameter holes along its center line. The holes begin 2" from each end and are centered 2" apart. Cut board N down the center after drilling the holes. The result will be two boards with "half" holes. Then as shown here, attach the boards using glue and 2" screws to the inside face of each back side. Position these notched boards so they both touch the bottom cross brace.

TIP

Use a small drill bit to locate the center of each hole in the side boards. Drill the 1" hole from both sides, meeting in the middle, to prevent tear-out and splintering at the hole edge.

STEP 13 The adjustable support arm is constructed with two sides (P), two position dowels (R), and two pivot blocks (Q). The pivot blocks require a 1"-diameter hole centered on the block. And the support arm sides require a 1"-diameter hole centered 1" from each end. The pivot blocks should rotate freely on each dowel, and the arms are "pinned" to the dowels with 1¼" screws. Then as shown here, install the support arm assembly by attaching the pivot blocks to the inside face of each side board. Position the blocks flush with the bottom edge of the sides and back against the legs. Use 2½" screws in pilot holes to secure the blocks.

STEP 14 Cut a 1"-wide slot, 12" long, in one side rail. The pullout can be installed on either side, so locate the slotted opening accordingly. The lower edge of the slot should be 1½" above the bottom edge of the side rail. Cut the slot between the center brace and headboard end of the lounge. The slot begins tight to the center brace. Use a 1"-diameter bit to drill holes at both ends of the slot and complete the cut with a jigsaw.

STEP 15 The pullout support is made with two upper runners (U), which are glued and nailed to the underside of the slats. The lower runners (T) are installed 1" below the upper runners. One runner is attached to the center brace, and the other is attached 1" below the upper runner using the pullout support cleats (S). The runners are spaced 12" apart in line with the side slot cutout. Use glue and brad nails to install the runners and cleats.

STEP 16 Build the pullout assembly as detailed. Attach the end caps (W) to the table boards (V) with glue and nails. Prepare both the pullout face (X) and handle (Y) by rounding over the edges. Then attach the pullout face to the table with glue and screws through the face into the end caps. Secure the handle with 2" screws in counterbored holes to the pullout face.

Construction Notes

- Since this is a heavy piece of furniture, it will probably remain outdoors all summer. That's a good reason to use the best exterior-rated adhesives, hardware and finishes.

- The only other option that might be of value is a set of wheels. You can cut wooden wheels with a jigsaw, sand them smooth, and attach them to the front legs with carriage bolts as the axles. But if you don't plan to move your chaise a great deal, the wheels might not be necessary.

- You may also want a thin mattress for your chaise. If you're not skilled at sewing, you can enlist the help of a friend. However, don't leave the mattress on the chaise, as moisture will build up on the underside and eventually ruin the mattress and slats.

- This chaise is long and should accommodate even the tallest of people. But it can easily be altered to suit anyone's needs. Simply lengthen or shorten the main rails and adjust for the number of slats required.

- One of my friends saw the lounge and wanted one of her own. It illustrates how popular this project will be with friends and family. You may be building a few, so keep that leg pattern handy.

STEP 17 Install a stop cleat (Z) to limit the travel of the pullout. Secure it to the underside of the pullout with screws about 14" back from the front. Finally, complete the final sanding and apply a good exterior paint or stain. I used Sikkens Cetol 1 #078 Natural to complete my chaise lounge.

A Picnic Of a Build

BY LAURA ANN ARNOLD

This simple table is at home in the dining room—or outdoors.

Supplies

2 bolts, ½" x 4"
12 bolts, ½" x 3"
14 nuts, ½"
28 washers, ½"
200 screws, 2½"

This table is a picnic to build with dimensional lumber, screws and bolts.

I'm usually not intimidated by undertaking projects. We need some artwork for the new apartment? I can paint some vivid, abstract oil paintings. Hair is not the way I wanted it? I'll trim it. Not the right color? I'll dye it. Shirt too loose? Hand-stitch it. We need a dining room table? Well … I'll drive us to Ikea.

The odd thing was, I shouldn't have been intimidated about making something. I'm not a fan of measurements, but I can use them when necessary. Making a picnic table is a large project, true, but it wasn't the size—or the numbers—that was intimidating.

It was the saws. And the splinters. What if I cut off a finger? What if I drilled through my palm like some sort of nightmarish woodshop stigmata scene? After telling my irrational and oddly descriptive fears to step aside, my husband, David, and I stepped into the *Popular Woodworking Magazine* shop.

We went over some safety tips, reviewed the design for the table and got to work.

The miter saw was the hardest thing for me to get over. Sure it looks innocent, but the idea of pulling the sharp, quickly rotating blade down and toward myself seemed foolish, if not downright dangerous. I discovered that the key was to go slow. Not only did this make it easier and give me more control, it also made for a much cleaner cut.

Making the Cuts

This picnic table is going to be our dining room table. After painting it black, I covered the tabletop with my favorite food and beer memorabilia I've collected as a food blogger, mostly six-pack covers. Then, to protect the stuff, we covered the tabletop with some thin Plexiglas. It looks great.

However, you might have different plans for your picnic table. Say, a picnic perhaps? In that case you'll want to purchase pressure-treated pine or a rot-resistant species, such as redwood (pricey!) or white oak (still pricey). We used white pine, which was cheap. You can use white pine as well, as long as you paint the table and maintain the paint job. Our table is going to live a long, cushy table life indoors.

The table requires about a dozen 2x6x8s, some 2½" screws and some hex-head bolts, washers and matching nuts. Oh, and you'll need a long afternoon or a few friends. I brought the beer—for after the work was done. Don't drink and drill.

ENDS ARE THE BEGINNING. Make the two end assemblies first. Then attach the top and diagonal braces.

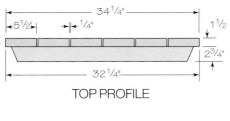

TOP PROFILE

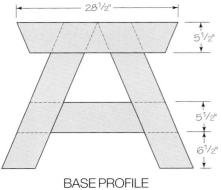

BASE PROFILE

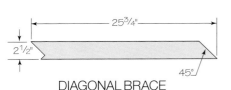

DIAGONAL BRACE

Schedule of Materials: Picnic Table

NO.	ITEM	DIMENSIONS (INCHES)			COMMENTS
		T	W	L	
6	Top pieces	1½	5½	8	
4	Legs	1½	5½	28¹¹/₁₆	22.5° Angle Both Ends
2	Upper braces	1½	5½	28½	22.5° Angle Both Ends
4	Narrow upper cleats	1½	2¾	32¼	22.5° Angle Both Ends
4	Lower braces	1½	5½	28½	22.5° Angle Both Ends
2	Diagonal braces	1½	2½	25¾	45° Angle Both Ends

SPACED OUT. Use shims to space out your top boards. When the top looks good, screw it down.

Odd Angle; Easy Cuts

To begin, pick out the six best 2x6s for the top and set them aside. Pick out the stock for your legs and set your miter saw's table to cut a 22.5° angle. Lock it there. Cut your legs to length (use a stop-block to make sure they're all the same size).

Design-wise, the table is better too short than too tall, especially if one of the members of your family is petite, like me. David is 6' plus and I'm 5'2" on a good day. It is easier for him adjust to a shorter table than for me to constantly strain upward. Now cut the bottom braces and top braces to length—they are identical and each end is cut at 22.5°.

After that, arrange each end assembly on your bench or garage floor. Place the legs so they touch at the top. Position the lower brace so the ends are flush to the legs and the legs touch at the top. Bolt the lower brace to the legs for each end assembly. Following that, place the top brace in place. Center it on legs and bolt it as well.

To make the narrower top cleats and diagonal braces, you'll need to rip one of your 2x6s. Once you rip it to width, cut the ends to 22.5° on the miter saw. Glue

and screw one narrow cleat to the top of each leg assembly. You'll have two narrow cleats left.

Attach the Top

To attach the top pieces, balance your end assemblies on the floor and space them 63" apart. Put clamps on the feet to stabilize them. Space the top pieces out on top of the legs. When they look good, screw them down. Flip (easy now) the whole assembled thing over so the feet are sticking in the air like road kill.

Now cut your diagonal braces. These have a 45° angle on each end. Set your miter saw to 45° and cut them to length. Then fit them between the end assemblies and top. When they fit, screw the two narrower top cleats (remember those?) to the underside of the top. Then screw each diagonal brace to each narrow top cleat.

Two Bolts for Strength

To ensure your picnic table lasts, you should bolt the diagonal brace to the end assembly. We used ½" x 4" hex-head bolts with washers and nuts. Drill a ½" clearance hole through each lower brace and through the diagonal brace (have a friend hold the diagonal brace while you drill the hole).

Now you need to cut a square notch in the diagonal brace so the washer and bolt have a flat area to sit on. Cut the notch with a handsaw and tighten the bolts.

Almost done! The last few steps are just sanding and finishing. Be sure to break all the sharp edges using #120-grit sandpaper. If you are painting the picnic table, you can sand the entire project up to #120-grit and call it a day. If you are going to add some sort of clear finish (such as a deck stain), go up to #150 grit.

Though it was a big project, our rewards were great. I should not have been afraid of detaching any digits. In fact, the only injury I sustained throughout the entire project was a paper cut—from the wrapping on my chicken fingers when we broke for lunch.

Now we need some bookshelves for the apartment. I can do that! Let's get started. I'll man the miter saw.

PROJECT 14

Greene & Greene
Garden Table

BY JIM STUARD

A classy piece that looks great on the patio or in your living room.

A reader from Claremont, California, Everett Vinzant, liked our Greene & Greene Garden Bench in the May '97 issue (#96) so much he decided to build a coffee table to go with it. He sent us a photo of it, and we decided it was such a good idea we tweaked his nice design and built this table. We call this project "Revenge of the Cloud Lifts" because it's loaded with this undulating signature Arts & Crafts detail. Because there are so many cloud lifts, this is a good project to use template routing on a router table to make them all.

Making Templates

Begin by cutting the parts out according to the Schedule of Materials. Then make your plywood templates using the patterns in the PullOut™ Plans. Mark a center line across each template. This will help you line up the parts for routing. Finish each template by adding two handles to the templates in the locations shown in the PullOut Plans.

Roughing the Parts

Mark a center line across parts B, C, D, F, G, K and on two top slats (J). Mark a center line down the middle and across parts E and K. These get a four-hole cutout. Make four copies of the small four-hole cutout and one of the larger four-hole patterns in the PullOut Plans. Cut the patterns to within ½" of the holes. Using a spray adhesive, attach the small patterns on the end uprights (E) and the large pattern on the center slat (K) lining up the cross hairs on the pattern with the cross hairs on the parts. Drill ¼" clearance holes in each hole and cut out the squares with a scroll saw. You can't quite cut all of the holes on the center slat but come close and clean up the rest with a chisel.

STEP ONE: MAKING TEMPLATES Begin cutting out the ½" Baltic Birch templates by drilling holes at the proper corners. Raise the blade on the table saw into the middle of the stock to make the straight cuts. Band saw the rest and clean up the cloud lifts using a disc sander.

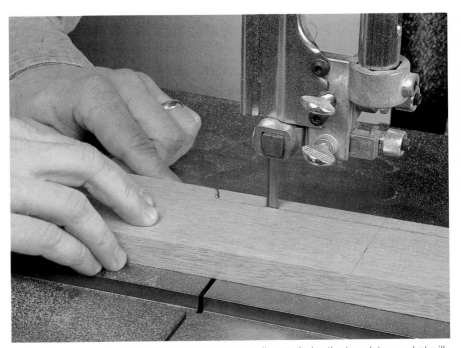

STEP TWO: ROUGHING OUT THE PARTS Use the center lines to index the template on what will be the back of each piece (it will eventually have nails driven into it) and draw the appropriate cloud lift or reverse cloud lift. Cutting close to the line, rough out these pieces on the band saw.

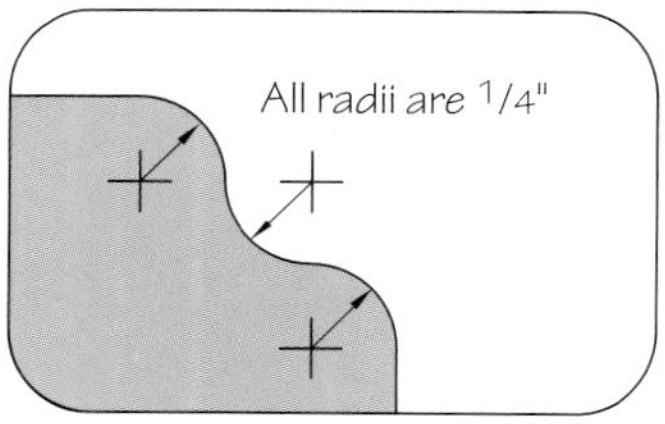
All radii are 1/4"

Full-size detail of corner profile

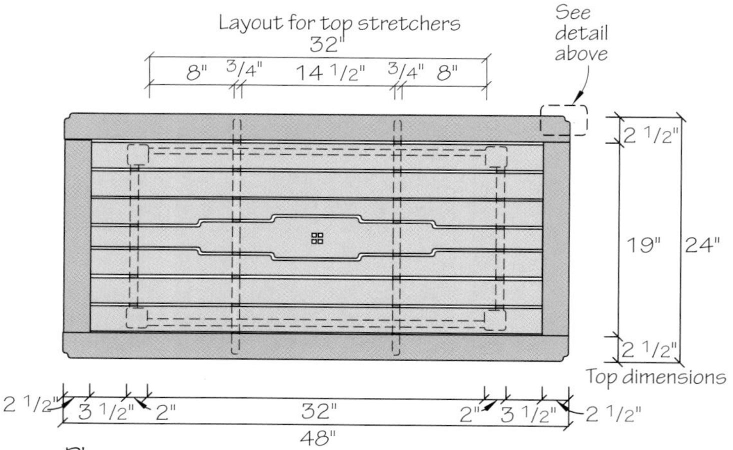
Layout for top stretchers
32"
8" 3/4" 14 1/2" 3/4" 8"
See detail above
2 1/2"
19"
24"
2 1/2"
Top dimensions
2 1/2" 3 1/2" 2" 32" 2" 3 1/2" 2 1/2"
48"

Plan

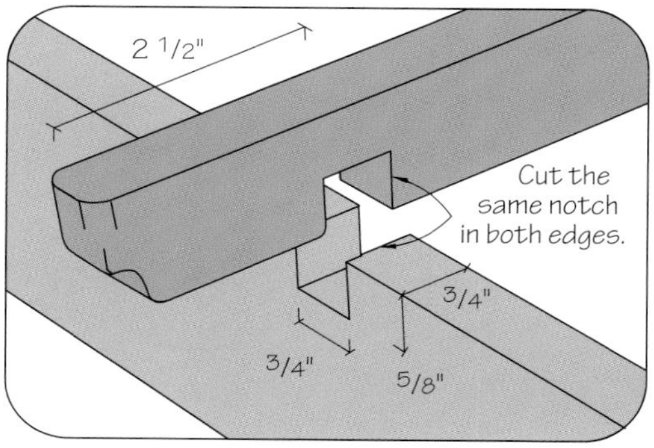
2 1/2"
Cut the same notch in both edges.
3/4"
3/4"
5/8"

Detail of top stretcher

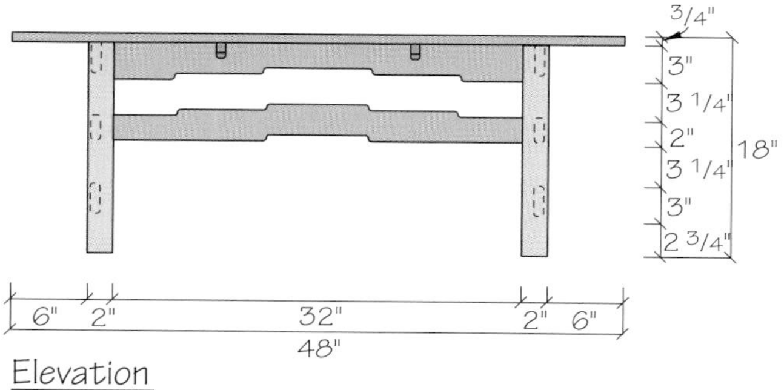
3/4"
3"
3 1/4"
2"
3 1/4"
3"
2 3/4"
18"
6" 2" 32" 2" 6"
48"

Elevation

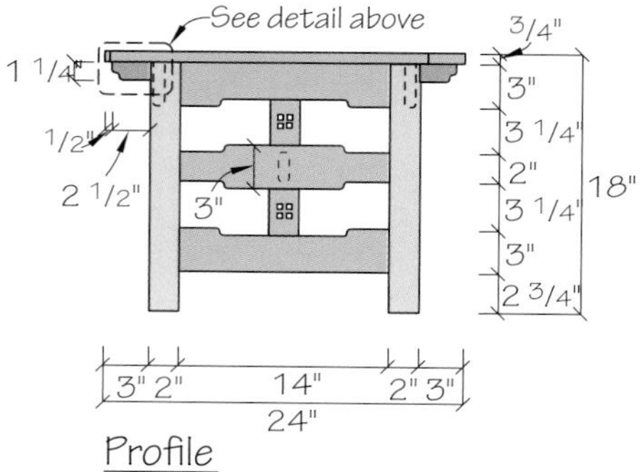
See detail above
1 1/4"
1/2"
2 1/2"
3"
3/4"
3"
3 1/4"
2"
3 1/4"
3"
2 3/4"
18"
3" 2" 14" 2" 3"
24"

Profile

Schedule of Materials: Greene Garden Table

NO.	LTR.	ITEM	DIMENSIONS (INCHES) T	W	L	MATERIAL
4	A	Legs	2	2	17¼	Mahogany
2	B	Long aprons	¾	3	32	Mahogany
4	C	Short aprons	¾	3	14	Mahogany
2	D	End divider	¾	3	14	Mahogany
4	E	End uprights	¾	2	3¼	Mahogany
1	F	Base stretcher	¾	3	34	Mahogany
2	G	Top stretchers	¾	1¼	23	Mahogany
2	H	Top frame long	¾	2½	48	Mahogany
2	I	Top frame short	¾	2½	19	Mahogany
6	J	Top slats	¾	2½	43	Mahogany
1	K	Center slat	¾	3	43	Mahogany

Routing the Parts

Mount a ⅜" pattern bit into a router table and set the depth of the bearing to run against the template while cutting the part.

Biscuits and Assembly

After routing the cloud lifts, cut all of the biscuit joints for the base and top. I used Porter-Cable's new biscuit joiner for this table because it comes with a 2" blade perfect for joining the base and top parts with smaller biscuits.

The easiest way to lay out the biscuit joints is to dry-clamp the end assembly together and mark the centers of the ends on the apron pieces and legs. The aprons have a ¼" setback from the outside of the legs, so cut the biscuit slots on the apron assembly first. Then, using a ¼" spacer, set up the biscuit joiner to cut the offset on the legs. Use #20 biscuits on the short aprons (C) and Porter-Cable face frame biscuits (or dowels) on the end dividers and uprights (D and E). Before assembly, rout a ¼" radius on the legs and the ends of the apron parts that contact the legs. Rout the rest of the assembly after gluing up. One last step before assembly is to drill screw pockets into the upper aprons for attaching the top. Glue up the end assembly.

After drying, mark the location of the base stretcher on each end assembly. Take the long aprons and base stretcher and dry clamp the entire base together. The base stretcher should be press fit between the end assemblies. Repeat the same process of cutting #20 biscuit slots on the long aprons and end assemblies.

PRO TIP

PIERCE CUT: Raising the table saw's blade through a part and lowering it when done. In solid lumber, this works only when making a rip cut. Man-made materials (such as MDF and plywood) can be ripped or crosscut.

CLIMB CUT: Slowly routing backwards from the cutting direction of a router bit. This will give a smoother cut in figured woods and when routing across end grain.

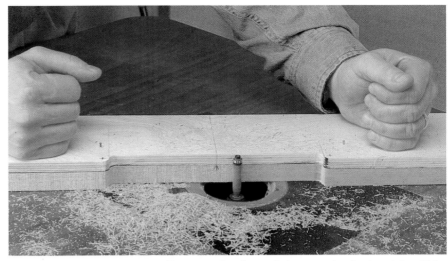

STEP THREE: ROUTING THE PARTS Pattern routing the parts is easy using the templates. Nail the appropriate template to a roughed out part, using the index lines for reference. Begin routing with the bit cutting against the wood. When you come to a cloud lift, use a climb cut so you don't burn the rounded corner.

STEP FOUR: NOTCHING THE STRETCHER Lay out a ⅝"-deep by ¾"-wide notch into the top stretcher and the base. The notch is 2¾" in from the stretcher end and 8" in from the joint where the apron meets the leg. Notice the clearance holes drilled into the top edge of the base and stretcher.

Dowel the base stretcher into each end assembly using two ⅜" dowels. After doweling the stretcher, lay out and scroll saw the profile on the ends of the top stretchers using the pattern in the PullOut Plans. Let the top stretchers into the base using half-lap joints according to the diagram. Then glue the entire base together and screw the stretchers into the top edge of the base.

Begin the top assembly by routing a ¼" radius on the top long edge of all the slats. Using ¼" spacers, clamp the slats together without glue. Dry clamp the ends in place and mark for biscuit joints. Cut the biscuit slots and glue this top sub-assembly together. When dry, place the long top frame pieces against the sub-assembly and mark the inside corner where the short frame meets the long frame. Rout a ¼" radius on the inside edge of the long frame piece between the corner marks. With a rasp, finish the radius where it tapers on the ends. Mark and cut biscuit slots, then glue up the top. After drying, cut a profile on each corner using the pattern for the top stretchers. Rout a ¼" radius on the outside edge of the top.

After sanding, center the base on the underside of the top and attach it to the top using 1½" screws in the screw pockets and 1¾" screws in the top stretchers. No finish is required. If you leave the table unfinished and outdoors, it will turn a beautiful silver color.

Greene and Greene Garden Table

Full-size diagram of the cloud lifts. Use this to lay out the individual cloud lifts on the jig above. Each square equals 1".

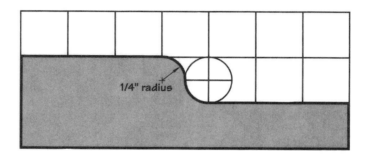

Greene and Greene Garden Table

Full-Size diagram of both four-hole cutouts, the double radius on the top stretcher and top, the layout for all of the cloud lifts on the table and a scale diagram of the jig used for routing the cloud lifts.

Top stretcher

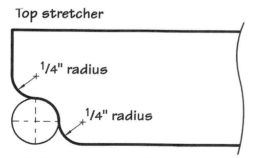

Full-size diagram of double radius on the top strecher and top

Top cutouts

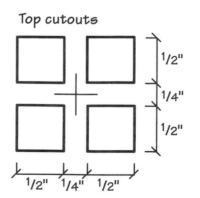

Full-size diagram of four hole cutouts inthe top and end assemblies

End assembly cutouts

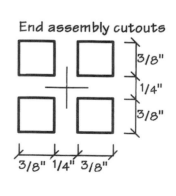

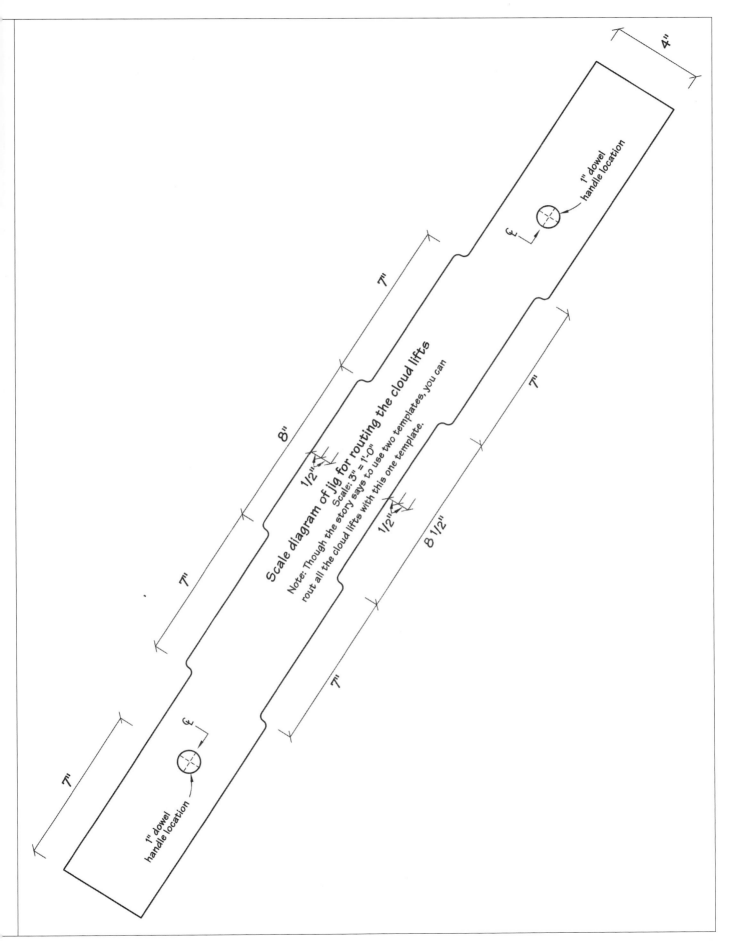

Scale diagram of jig for routing the cloud lifts
Scale: 3" = 1'-0"
Note: Though the story says to use two templates, you can rout all the cloud lifts with this one template.

1" dowel handle location

1" dowel handle location

4"

7"

8"

1/2"

7"

7"

1/2"

7"

8 1/2"

℄

℄

Outdoor Table

BY DAVID THIEL

This outdoor dining table is a fairly straightforward trestle design that is seen in a variety of Arts & Crafts pieces.

Designed to seat four, the dimensions could be extended slightly to accommodate six. All that would be required would be to extend the length of the lower stretchers and add another stretcher at the top for stability. The top would need to be lengthened by about 20", but other than that, the option is there.

As this is an outdoor piece, I've used pine for construction, but the piece could be built from oak and finished with an indoor stain and top coat. For more formal use, the top slats could be replaced with a piece of oak veneer plywood, also available at your home center store.

There are a lot of pieces to this project, so it's best to think of it in two main sections: the base and the top. The base itself is made up of three parts; the two legs and the stretcher that runs between the legs. And just to make things interesting, the legs are actually built in halves and then glued together to add mass and stability to the whole base.

The Legs & Stretcher

Construction starts with marking the corner notch cuts necessary on the four tops (supports) and four bottoms (bracket feet) of the legs. The cuts are identical and can all be made at the same time.

The four bracket feet also have an arch cut in the lower edge that is made with a jigsaw.

With the bracket and support cuts made, the stretcher that provides stability to the lower portion of the base is screwed together.

One of the tricks with this table was hiding as much of the joinery as possible. Because of this, the legs are screwed to the stretcher and bracket halves from the inside, creating two half-assemblies that are then biscuited and glued together.

The inner brackets are first screwed to the stretcher, then the legs are screwed in place on the brackets. The inner supports are then screwed in place against the legs.

The outer half of the leg assemblies are screwed together separately and then the two halves are glued together to form the completed legs. The biscuits are used to align the two halves of the leg posts to keep things straight and to reduce sanding and clean-up work of sloppy joints.

The Top

The top was also a little interesting in that I didn't want to add a rabbet ledge

to the frame to support the top slats. Trying to figure a way to keep things level and at a ¾" thickness was interesting, but ultimately not too hard. The top consists of a ¾"-thick eight-sided frame that is biscuited together at the joints. This required both 45° and 22.5° miter cuts. I was able to use my miter saw, but if that tool isn't available to you, a circular saw and a good protractor will do.

The frame itself is inadequate to provide enough support for the top, so I designed it with the first slat in from either side glued and biscuited to the long frame edge and the two frame corner pieces. This provides a solid support to the frame. The middle section is then glued in place between the two rigid outside lengths, and then the top is screwed to the upper supports on the table legs, holding everything in place. I plugged the four holes in the top slats and sanding everything smooth, adding a roundover profile to the upper and lower edges of the top.

A couple of coats of a flat exterior-grade paint finished the table up, and it was ready for the party.

While the photo shows a "solid" top, I wanted to add a standard table umbrella, and did this easily enough by screwing a

3½" × 3½" square plate to the underside of the top slats, dead center on the table. A hole saw sized to fit my umbrella made the hole through the top easily. I then inserted the umbrella, squared the pole to the tabletop, and marked the location on the lower stretcher. Another minute with the hole saw and a

second hole was cut through the lower stretcher.

These two holes stabilized the umbrella adequately, but if you want to avoid the umbrella turning in a breeze, a simple screw through the side of the lower stretcher and into the umbrella pole will do the trick.

Schedule of Materials: Outdoor Table

LTR.	NO.	ITEM	STOCK	INCHES T	(MM) T	INCHES W	(MM) W	INCHES L	(MM) L
A	8	legs	pine	¾	(19)	3½	(89)	28¼	(718)
B	8	supports/brackets	pine	¾	(19)	3½	(89)	23	(584)
C	2	stretchers	pine	¾	(19)	3½	(89)	20	(508)
D	2	top frame	pine	¾	(19)	3½	(89)	40	(1016)
E	2	top frame	pine	¾	(19)	3½	(89)	8½	(216)
F	2	top frame	pine	¾	(19)	3½	(89)	18	(457)
G	6	top slats	pine	¾	(19)	3½	(89)	45	(1143)

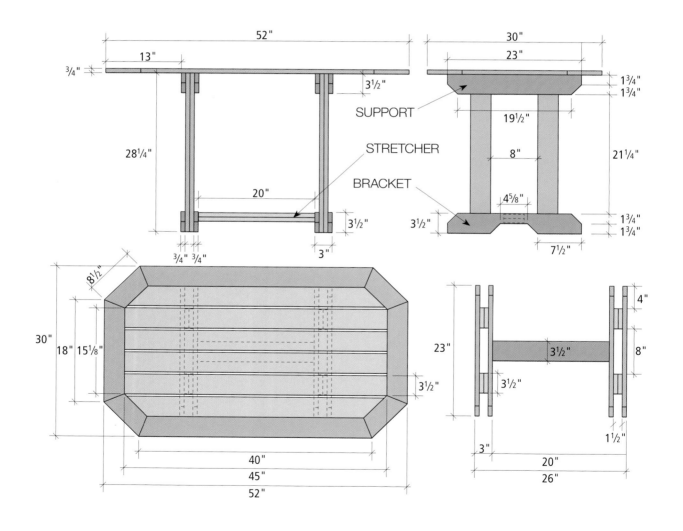

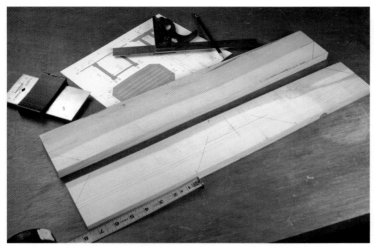

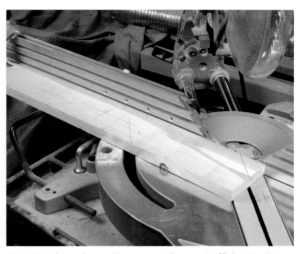

STEP ONE Mark the location of the corner bevels on the four upper supports and the four base pieces, and also mark the lower "arch" on the base pieces.

STEP TWO I used my miter saw as the most efficient tool to cut the bevels on the corners of the eight pieces, but this could also be easily accomplished with a jigsaw.

STEP THREE I did use my jigsaw to first define both sides of the lower arches.

STEP FOUR I next cut a sweeping curve from the center of the arch to one of the corners, allowing the waste piece to drop free. I then cut from the open space along the top edge of the arch to the other corner. Both waste pieces are shown here, with only a little trimming at the top of the arch to finish the cut.

STEP FIVE The center beam or stretcher is made of two pieces of 3½"-wide material glued and screwed together from the underside. Since this piece is painted and this is the underside, I didn't bother to countersink the screws.

STEP SIX On the inner feet brackets, I marked the approximate location of where the lower beam would intersect the bracket. I started to mark and drill for only two screws, but decided there was enough room for four.

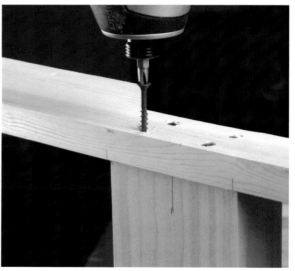

STEP SEVEN I used 2½"-long screws to attach the inner bracket feet. I didn't countersink or plug these holes on my table, but were I to do it over, I think I'd take that step the second time around, as these were the only visible (but fairly well hidden) screws when the table was complete.

STEP EIGHT I then set the base frame on my work surface and made sure it was sitting flat before screwing the second inner bracket foot in place.

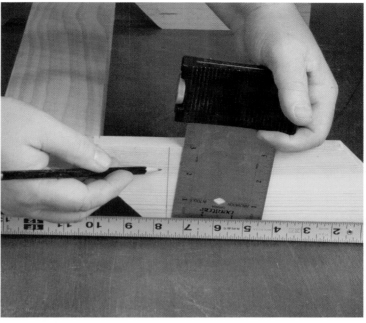

STEP NINE Moving on to the posts for the legs, I marked biscuit locations for six biscuits (three per edge) along the post-piece edges. I found it easier to make this cut with two of the pieces held together to provide more bearing surface during the cut.

STEP TEN I next moved back to the bracket foot assembly and marked perpendicular lines on the feet to indicate the post locations. By the way, I love my Veritas Sliding Square for this type of work (www.leevalley.com).

STEP 11 Starting with one end, I screwed one post in place with four screws, then put only one screw in the second post.

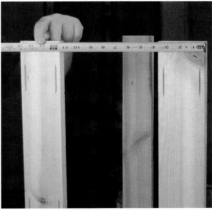

STEP 12 I measured across the two posts down by the feet, and then made sure that the dimension was the same at the top of the posts, then put the last three screws in the bottom of that post.

STEP 13 I then screwed the top supports in place at the top of the posts. Both sets of posts and the inner supports are shown here.

STEP 14 Moving to the outer halves of the posts/feet/supports, I first marked the post locations on the remaining upper supports and bracket feet, making sure the lines were perpendicular to the bottom of the feet brackets.

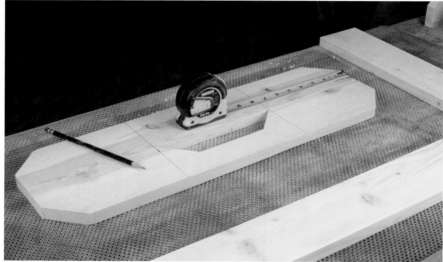

STEP 15 I then screws the second half of the posts to the top supports only, again checking squareness as I moved forward.

STEP 17 After disassembling the post halves, I finished screwing the posts to the outer bracket feet from the inside face of the post halves.

STEP 16 To double check the alignment, I put a couple of biscuits (without glue) in place in each half of the posts and pushed the two halves together. I then marked the post location on the outer bracket feet.

STEP 18 The assembled outer leg sections were then glued in place with the biscuits all in their slots for proper alignment. They really do make things easier during a large glue-up.

STEP 19 Work on a flat surface to make sure the feet brackets rest evenly on the surface. Depending on the number of clamps you have available, you may need to do one side, and then the other.

STEP 20 I made a squareness guide on my work surface to help me lay out and cut all the miters for the top pieces. Start with the squared corner, then work around the outside of the frame, finally filling in the center slats.

STEP 21 Assembly starts with one long frame piece and the adjoining two corner pieces. Fit the first slat into that space once the frame is established, then mark and cut for biscuits.

STEP 22 Glue and clamp these piece together following this same pattern (outside frame first, first slat, then corners) to assemble the one side of the frame. Then repeat this process for the opposite side of the top frame.

STEP 23 Mark the biscuit locations for the four middle slats on the two short frame pieces, but don't glue this up yet.

STEP 24 When the outer frame sections are dry, mark the biscuit locations joining the outer sections and the short frame pieces.

STEP 25 Start assembling the top by gluing one outer frame section to the middle section.

STEP 26 Then add the other outer frame section, tapping and clamping the frame into place to adjust all the joints as you go. Clamp it tight and let it dry.

Dining Table & Stools

BY JIM STACK

Dining *al fresco* is easy with this simple and functional dining set.

A round table seats more people than a square table with the same overall dimensions. This table will probably be the only table you'll need if you have a small cabin. It can be used for food preparation, eating, playing board games and a general catchall. The stools provide very flexible seating and can be pushed under the table, completely out of the way, if more room is needed.

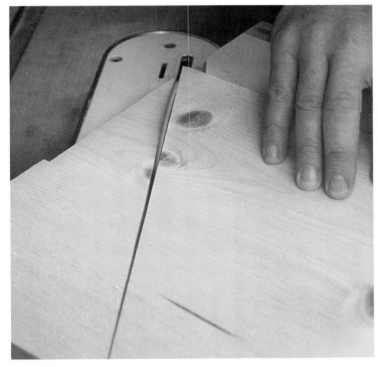

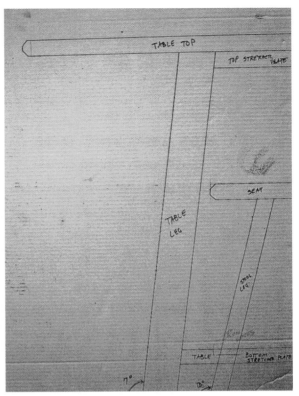

STEP ONE It is recommended that a full-scale elevation of the table and stools be drawn so all angles may be accurately transferred to the parts.

STEP TWO Here you'll cut the triangle-shaped stretcher panel for the table and stool bases. After laying out the triangle to determine how large you need to make your stretcher panel blanks (see sidebar "Drawing an Equilateral Triangle"), glue up the blanks as squares, set the table saw miter gauge on 30° and make the first cut.

STEP THREE After cutting all the parts per the materials list, make a simple dowling jig from a scrap piece that will hold the drill bit at the proper angle when drilling the dowel holes for the table leg/stretcher panel joint.

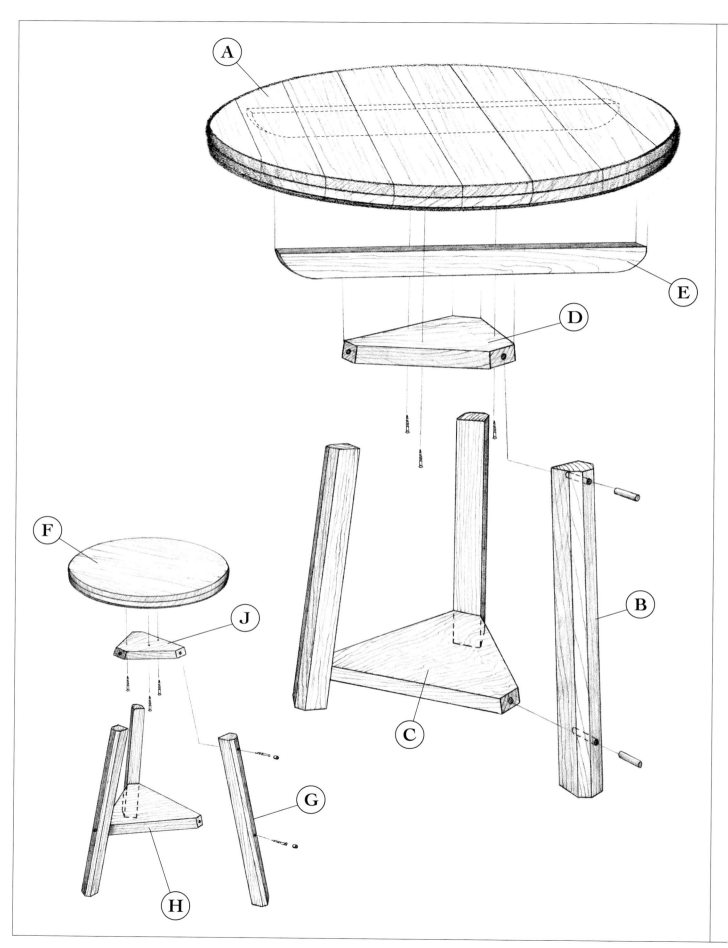

Schedule of Materials: Dining Table & Stools

NO.	LTR.	ITEM	DIMENSIONS (INCHES)			MATERIAL	COMMENTS
			T	W	L		
TABLE							
A	1	Top	1³/₈	40 dia.		Sugar Pine	
B	3	Legs	2¾	2¾	28	Sugar Pine	w/ 7° angles on each end
C	1	Bottom Brace	1¼	15¼	17⅝	Sugar Pine	w/ 7° angles at each clipped corner
D	1	Top Brace	1¼	11¼	12¾	Sugar Pine	w/ 7° angles at each clipped corner
E	2	Battens	1¼	2	26	Sugar Pine	w/ radius at each end
STOOLS							
F	1	Top	1¼	13½ dia.		Sugar Pine	
G	3	Legs	1¼	1¼	16¾	Sugar Pine	w/ 13½° angles on each end
H	1	Bottom Brace	1	8	9¼	Sugar Pine	w/ 13½° angles at each clipped corner
J	1	Top Brace	1	4½	5¼	Sugar Pine	w/ 13½° angles at each clipped corner

Note: Double-check the angle measurements on the table and the stools by drawing a full-scale elevation. This will save time and materials.

Drawing an Equilateral Triangle

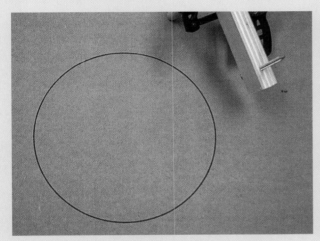

STEP ONE First draw a circle with the diameter you've chosen.

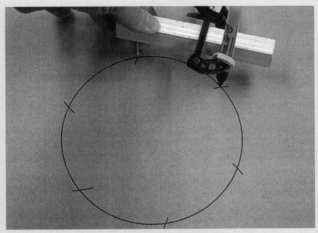

STEP TWO Next, keeping the compass set to the radius, set the center on the circle line and strike a point on the circle. Continue doing this around the circle, dividing the circle into six equal sections.

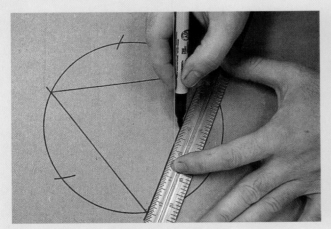

STEP THREE Then connect every other point you drew on the circle.

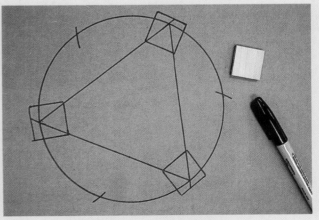

STEP FOUR Finally, determine the leg size and draw it at the triangle points. This will give you a full-size template for the connecting braces for the table and stools.

STEP FOUR Flip over the blank and make the second cut.

STEP FIVE To clip the ends of the triangle, reset the miter gauge to 30° on the other side of the gauge and set the blade to the required leg-splay angle. Hold the panel against the fence and cut off the end of the tri-angle. This creates the joint surface for the legs.

STEP SIX Glue on one leg at a time. Note the use of angled clamp blocks. One clamp attaches to each side of the block. This evens out the clamping pressure applied to the leg/stretcher joint.

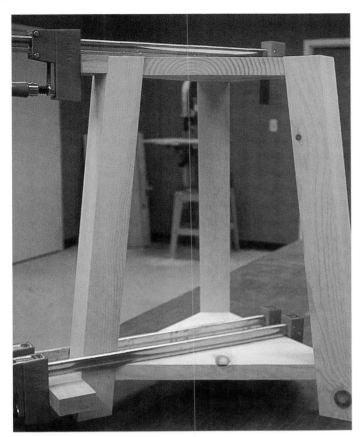

STEP SEVEN Flip over the blank and make the second cut.

TIP

This is another method for making the table or stool base. Tilt your band saw table to the angle of leg splay and cut out a disc. Sand the edge and attach the legs with dowels or screws.

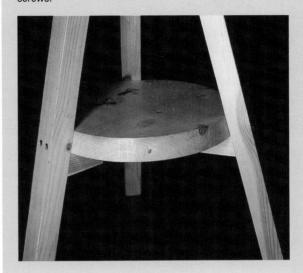

STEP EIGHT To soften the shape of the legs, rout a 45° angle on the two outside corners of the legs.

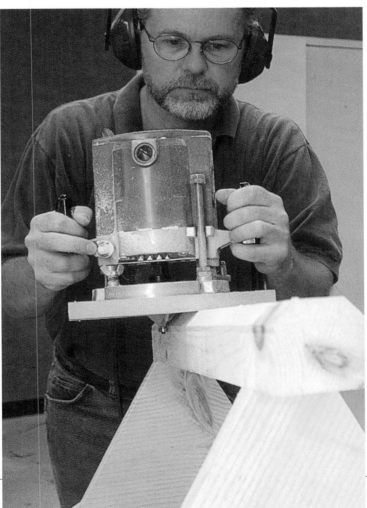

STEP NINE It's easy to cut circles on the band saw. After the top and seat blanks have been glued up to size, mark a center on the blank and drill a hole at this mark on the bottom of the blank.

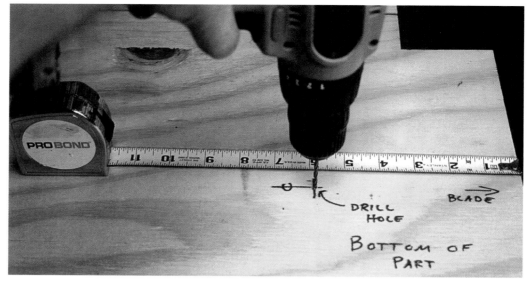

STEP TEN This illustrates the proper setup of the circle-cutting jig on the band saw.

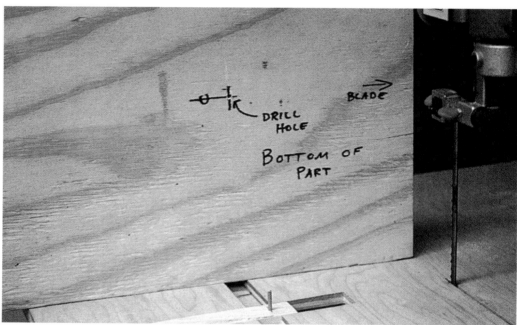

STEP 11 Complete the circle cutout, and sand the edges of the top pieces. Rout a 45° bevel on the top and bottom edges.

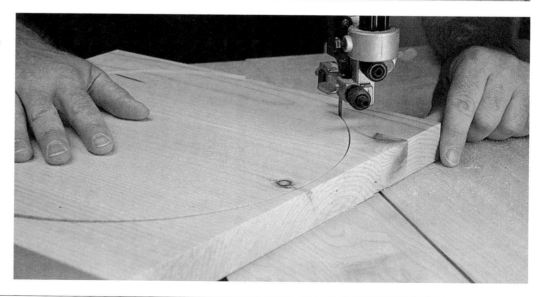

STEP 12 Drill oversize holes in the top brace and attach the top (seat) pieces with screws. Do not use any glue.

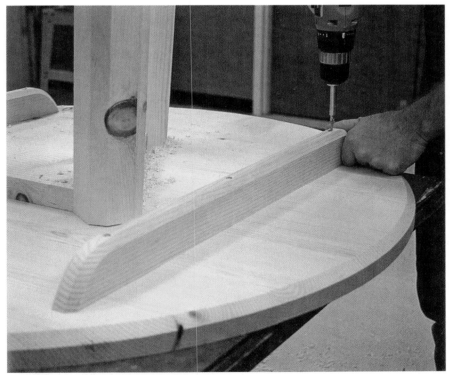

STEP 14 Stain the projects (if you choose) the color of your choice. Let the stain dry for half a day and apply the finish of your choice. These particular stools were stained dark and finished with three coats of pre-catalyzed lacquer.

STEP 13 Cut out the two battens, round the ends and bevel the two long edges. Drill oversize holes in the battens and, using screws, attach them across the grain of the top. These battens will keep the top flat while allowing it to move according to changes in moisture. Again, do not use any glue.

Old Plane Birdhouse

BY CHRISTOPHER SCHWARZ

Every woodworker should spruce up the yard (or the shop) with this simple birdhouse.

I've never been a fan of birdhouses. Why welcome something to your yard that really wants to poo on your head?

Yet, inspiration works in weird ways. While visiting Maine in February I saw an enormous birdhouse that looked like a jointer plane hanging outside Liberty Tool, an ironmonger. I just had to have one to hang above my shop door.

Simple, Quick & Fun

This birdhouse is based on a Marples 14" razee jack plane I own. I scaled it up to 35" long so it would look good above a standard door. If you'd like to make yours bigger, you can scale our model by downloading the free SketchUp file through our web site.

You'll need about 10 to 12 board feet of a weather-resistant wood. I used cypress. And don't forget the waterproof glue and stainless (or galvanized) fasteners.

The whole project takes about three hours, so it also was great therapy for me after coming off of an intense three-month-long project.

Begin by gluing up the wood for the thick wedge and the tote. These pieces are made by gluing two pieces of stock face-to-face. Clamp them up and set them aside for the glue to dry.

Schedule of Materials:
Old Plane Birdhouse

NO.	ITEM	DIMENSIONS (INCHES)		
		T	W	L
2	Sidewalls	¾	6½	35
1	Toe	¾	5	6½
1	Top	¾	5	8
1	Front of mouth	¾	5	5
1	Frog	¾	5	3½
1	Plate for tote	¾	5	17½
1	Divider	¾	5	3¼
1	Heel	¾	5	4¾
1	Sole	¾	5	33½
1	Tote	1½	7½	10
1	Wedge	1½	5	9¼
1	Iron	½	5	18

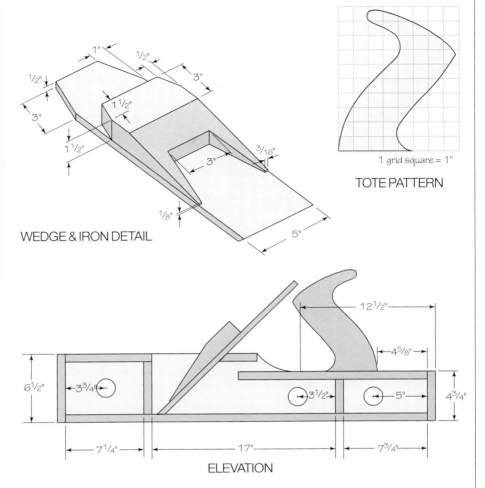

WEDGE & IRON DETAIL

1 grid square = 1"

TOTE PATTERN

ELEVATION

Next Up: The Sidewalls

After ripping all your parts to width, begin by shaping the two sidewalls. Lay out the razee shape on one sidewall using the drawing as a guide. Cut the shape on the band saw and clean it up with a spindle sander. Then use the first sidewall to lay out the pattern for the second.

Cut that one close, then tape the two sidewalls together and shape them simultaneously so they are identical. I used the spindle sander here as well.

Assembly. What, Already?

Cut the interior parts to size: the toe, heel, top, front of the mouth, frog, divider and sole. Sand or plane them smooth, then get your nails out.

Glue and nail these seven pieces to the sidewall that will eventually have the entrances for the birds (you'll bore those holes later).

Now shape the tote. Remove the thick piece that you glued up earlier from the clamps and cut it to size using the patterns and drawings provided above. Dress it smooth and then screw the tote to the plate for the tote. Glue and nail the finished assembly to the sidewall.

Shape the iron and the wedge using the drawings to guide you. Glue and nail them in place to the sidewall and the frog.

Be Bird-friendly

Drill some ventilation and drainage holes in the sole and in the top of the plane using a ¼" bit. Then decide what sort of birds you want to attract and drill entrance holes that are based on the species (a quick search on the Internet will call up the hole sizes for a variety of birds). I want to attract Purple Martins, so I drilled my holes at 1⅞" in diameter.

So that the birdhouse is easy to clean, attach the second sidewall to your birdhouse using No. 8 x 1¼" stainless screws.

To hang the birdhouse, I made a French cleat. One half gets screwed to the sidewall. Its mate gets screwed to the house, right above my shop door.

And what about having the birdhouse hanging over my shop door? That seems stupid. Maybe. But perhaps the threat of some loose-boweled birds will prevent my neighbors from pestering me when I'm working in the shop.

THIS PLANE IS HOLLOW. Glue and nail all the interior pieces as shown before you screw the second sidewall in place.

Purple Martin Condo

BY A. J. HAMLER

This home for purple martins is one of the easiest and fastest projects in this book. And, because if its modular nature, it's also one of the most unique.

Purple martins are social nesters, and while individual birds prefer to have their "own room," so to speak, they enjoy living in colonies with other purple martins. Further, of all the cavity-nesting birds discussed throughout this book, purple martins rely the most on man-made housing; in fact, they prefer it to natural cavities, which often do not lend themselves to large colonies. With this house's design, you can not only make your purple martin colony as large as you'd like, your options for its final appearance are limitless based on how you arrange the finished modules.

Each module is based on the purple martin's preferred living space, a cube with minimum interior dimensions of 6" × 6" × 6", and is made entirely of ½" pine. Of course, you could substitute any other solid wood species, or even plywood.

Because you will likely make this house in multiple modules, it's best to cut multiples of each component at the same time to cut down on the number

of tool setups. That is, cut all the house backs with one setup, change your saw's setting and cut all the sides, change it again to cut all the fronts, etc. With the exception of the top/bottom components, all the house parts are very similar in size, so label your stacks as in Fig. 1 to keep everything straight.

With waterproof glue and nails, begin the assembly by attaching the house sides to the house back. To this assembly, attach the top and bottom pieces. (Fig. 2.) Drill a 2" entrance hole 2" on-center from the bottom of the house front/ door, then center the door in the front opening of the house and drive galvanized hinge nails on each side about an inch from the top. Notice that I've sized the front/door a bit smaller than the back, allowing for a narrow gap at both top and bottom when it's centered in the front opening. The bottom gap will allow for drainage, while both top and bottom gaps provide additional ventilation and allow the door to be easily lifted without rubbing at the top and bottom of the house. In Fig. 3 I'm using a nail set to put the heads of the hinge nails slightly below the surface. Finally, drill a pilot hole through one side and into the door near the bottom of the house, and drive in a 1" exterior screw to keep the door shut. Countersink the screw so it is flush with the house side.

Taking the number of modules you've made into consideration, you

Schedule of Materials: Purple Martin Condo

LTR.	NO.	ITEM	STOCK	INCHES T	(MM) T	INCHES W	(MM) W	INCHES L	(MM) L
A	1	back	pine	½	(13)	6	(152)	6	(152)
B	1	front/door	pine	½	(13)	6	(152)	5⅞	(149)
C	2	sides	pine	½	(13)	6	(152)	7	(178)
D	2	top/bottom	pine	½	(13)	7	(178)	8½	(216)

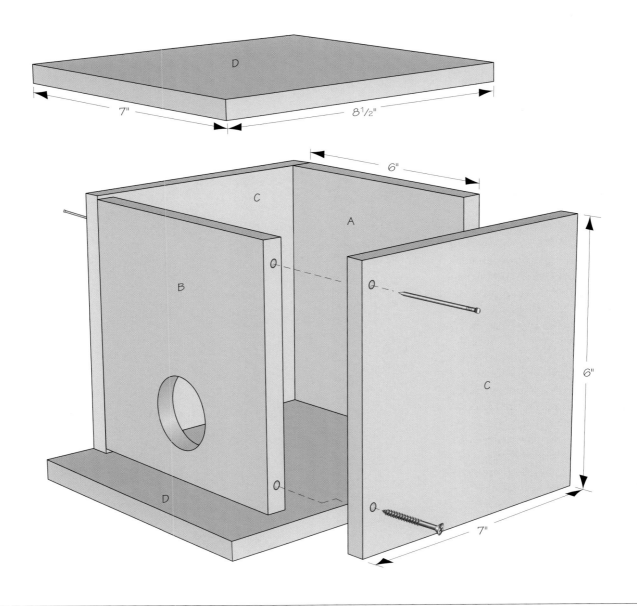

FIGURE 1 With the exception of the top/bottom components, which are identical, all the house parts are very similar in size, so label your stacks to keep everything straight.

FIGURE 2 With waterproof glue and nails, begin the assembly by attaching the house sides to the house back. To this assembly, attach the top and bottom pieces.

FIGURE 3 Use a nail set to put the heads of the hinge nails slightly below the surface.

can arrange them any way you'd like. (If you know what arrangement you'll use beforehand, place the door screw on the side of the house that will be most accessible in your arrangement.) The modules can be attached directly to each other with nails or screws, or can be individually attached to a plywood platform for low arrangements, or to a backer board for tall ones.

Your purple martin condo should be mounted on a pole 8' to 20' above the ground, and at least 35' to 40' from your house. Ideally, your home will be adjacent to a large field where purple martins will swoop through the air over large open areas to catch insects. This is important—their entire diet is caught this way—so if your home is surrounded by a lot of trees, it's really not the best location for a purple martin house.

Purple martins are the largest species of swallow in North America, and are common throughout the eastern, central, and portions of the Southwestern United States, as well as throughout Mexico and Central America. Deep black with a shimmering blue/purple sheen to the feathers, they're the only swallows without a light-colored underside. They feed entirely on insects, and so are migratory. Although they winter in South America, they will often return to the same northern nesting grounds they used the previous year.

Bat House

BY A. J. HAMLER

Bats aren't birds, of course, but in spite of the fact that they're among the most beneficial animals you can attract to your yard, they still get a bum rap.

Sure, they aren't cuddly or attractive (up close, in fact, you won't find anything uglier), but they earn their keep in two important ways. First, they put a huge big dent in local insect populations, especially mosquitoes. A single bat can, depending on size and species habit, eat several hundred insects an hour. The common little brown bat regularly downs as many as 20 insects per minute—that's a whopping 1,200 bugs an hour. The second benefit is derived from the first. Because lots of insects hang around flowering plants and trees, bats are also great pollinators. Birds perform both of those jobs, but the majority of insect-eating birds are strictly day-timers, meaning that bats take up the same job on the night shift for round-the-clock benefits.

This project is made entirely of ¾" cedar. A major difference between this house and the others in this book is that this one has a central divider separating the house into two sleep chambers. Also, in other house projects I've recommended orienting the rough face inward on the front to give a climbing surface to nestlings, but since bats don't just sleep at the bottom—they'll be climbing every interior surface of this house looking for a place to hang while they snooze—you should orient all the components with

the rough side facing in.

Bats don't need much room. I've designed this house for the little brown bat, the most common bat throughout the U.S. and Canada, so the sleeping chambers are a mere ¾". You can easily adjust dimensions for other bat species.

The best way to construct this house is front-to-back. Cut the house components to size. Like many of the houses in this book, the top is sloped at 10° to allow for better rain runoff, so the top of each side is cut at that angle, while the top edges of the house front and back are beveled at 10°. These cuts can be made with a miter saw, handsaw, or a table saw with a miter gauge.

Use a pencil to mark the inside surfaces of the sides for placement of the divider and house front, as in Fig. 1. I find marking in this way helps me keep parts straight, and facilitates locating them correctly when gluing and nailing. Since all the components are of the same thickness as the sleeping chambers, you can use an extra piece of scrap 3/4" stock to do your marking.

All the inner surfaces should be the rough faces of the cedar. Before construction, you'll need to roughen up the smooth face of the divider. The easiest way to do this is to clamp the divider to a work surface and score it repeatedly

with a utility knife. Note in Fig. 2 that I'm keeping my free hand behind that clamp at one end for safety.

Begin construction by attaching the front to the inside edge of one of the sides with glue and nails, followed by the center divider. Keeping the divider in place on your marks while you nail can be difficult, so instead install the divider with glue and clamps only as in Fig. 3. (We'll throw a couple reinforcing nails in there later.) The divider should be placed 2¾" from the bottom edge of the side workpiece; once the floor and roof are in place, this will create a 2" gap at both top and bottom of the sleeping chambers for the bats to maneuver inside the house.

When dry, remove the clamps and set the house on its completed side. Run beads of glue on the edges of the house front and divider, position the remaining side, and nail in place. (Fig. 4) At this point, you can place a couple nails through the sides and into the divider on the other side for a bit of added strength.

Hold the floor in place at the bottom of the house without glue, drill a single countersunk pilot hole on each side and secure the floor in place with screws as in Fig. 5. This will allow you to remove the floor for cleaning, which you will need to do periodically. While nesting birds frequently remove droppings from their houses, bats don't.

Attach the slanted roof with glue and nails, then mount the entire house on the back board, driving nails from the rear of the house. Finally, drill a ¼" to ⅜" ventilation hole near the top on each side.

Mount your bat house high on the side of a building, under the eaves if possible where it'll be out of the weather. Or, you can attach it to a tall pole; wooden telephone or utility lighting poles are excellent choices. Bats like a warm place to sleep, so orient the house facing east; this way, the house will warm quickly when the bats head home at dawn.

The main variation you can make with this house is size. Remember that bats will easily fill an entire cave, so there's really no upper limit. Just keep in mind that larger houses require very sturdy mounting, and will need more frequent cleaning. For larger bats, increase the size of the sleeping chamber and the house's bottom entrance. For the little brown bat, an entrance of ⅞" to 1" works well; larger bats need larger entrances. Also, no matter how large the house is, remember to build it so the back extends at least 6" below the house's bottom entrance, providing a landing area for bats to grasp before climbing up inside for the night… er, I mean day.

Schedule of Materials: Bat House

LTR.	NO.	ITEM	STOCK	INCHES T	(MM) T	INCHES W	(MM) W	INCHES L	(MM) L
A	2	sides	cedar	¾	(19)	3½	(89)	23½	(597)
B	1	front	cedar	¾	(19)	7½	(190)	23	(584)
C	1	divider	cedar	¾	(19)	7½	(190)	19½	(495)
D	1	floor	cedar	¾	(19)	1¾	(45)	7½	(190)
E	1	back	cedar	¾	(19)	9	(229)	30	(762)
F	1	roof	cedar	¾	(19)	6	(152)	12	(305)

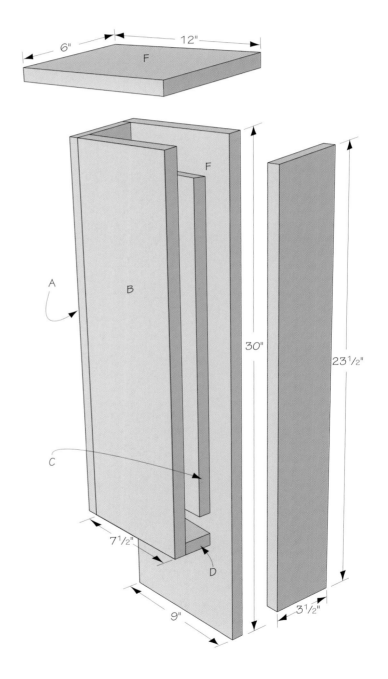

FIGURE 1 On the sides, lay out the location of the central divider and front and back.

FIGURE 2 When you're scoring the divider, keep your free hand clear of the blade.

FIGURE 3 It's a little easier to install the divider using just glue and some clamps. A couple of reinforcing nails can be added later.

FIGURE 4 Glue and nail the sides in place.

FIGURE 5 Secure the bottom in place with two screws only. You'll need to remove the bottom from time to time for cleaning.

Butterfly House

BY A. J. HAMLER

Like the bats discussed in the previous chapter, butterflies are natural pollinators. Unlike the flying mammals, however, butterflies are beautiful and brighten any yard or garden they frequent.

Attracting butterflies to your home by planting flowers they like is the first step in enticing them to take up residence. The other half is giving them a place to stay.

Some butterfly species—monarchs, mourning cloaks, longwings and tortoiseshells, for example—can live from several months to a full year. As a result, they address cold weather a couple different ways. Some migrate to warmer climates, finding shelter at night while they travel; others stay where they are and hibernate. But most butterflies, whether traveling or staying put, look for shelter during colder seasons, and even on chillier summer and fall nights. In the wild they'll look for crevices in trees or rocks. You can provide them shelter with a butterfly house—and at the same time add an attractive touch to your garden.

Butterfly houses can be almost any size, although about 3" square and 12" tall would be a good minimum. I've used ½" pine for the house here, but any untreated wood up to ¾" is fine. I like the look of unfinished wood, especially after it begins to weather, so I've left this one natural, but painted houses provide an additional splash of color to your landscaping. (Some butterfly aficionados insist that painting flowers on the houses attracts more butterflies, but the claim is difficult to quantify.)

Once again, I've used a 10° angle for the roof slope, but instead of cutting angles and bevels first, this house is small enough to do that slope another, easier way later in the construction process. For that reason, note that the vertical components are all the same length.

The most complicated part of this house is the front with its multiple ½" × 3¼" entrance slots. Mark the front for slot locations, starting with the middle one centered left-to-right, and 5¼" from the bottom. All four of the outer entrances are set in 1½" from the side edges. The two lower entrances are 1" from the bottom edge, while the two upper ones are 2" from the top edge. (Once the roof is sloped, all holes will be evenly centered on the house front.)

Start the entrance slots by drilling a ½" hole at each end, then clamp the workpiece to a secure surface and use a jigsaw to connect the holes, as in Fig. 1. Sand all the entrance edges smooth.

Butterflies like a natural, rough surface to cling to, and there are a couple ways you can do this. A large strip of solid bark the size of the sides can be glued or stapled in place like wallpaper on one or both sides of the house. I opted for halving some branches on the band saw, and stapling them in place as shown in Fig. 2. Since we'll be cutting the roof slope later, be sure the highest staple is placed at least 1½" from the top.

Attach the front of the house to the two sides with glue and nails, then attach the back the same way. Again, upper nails should be at least 1½" from the top edge to avoid cutting through them in the next step. Mark a cutline for the roof slope, and cut the 10° angle on your marks with a band saw or other saw, as in Fig. 3, and sand as necessary. You can make the roof angle steeper or shallower if you like. For that matter, you can eliminate the angle and go with a flat roof if you prefer.

Attach the roof with glue and nails. Make the bottom removable for cleaning by mounting it to the house with four screws, one through each side as in Fig. 4. When it comes to keeping a clean home, butterflies could win the Good Housekeeping award. However, leaves and other debris can get into the house through the multiple entrances, plus bark can deteriorate over time and you may wish to replace it.

Locate your finished butterfly house near your flowers, as a ready source of nectar will attract the butterflies to the area. The house should be mounted on a slender post driven into the ground, but should be no more than a foot or two off the ground. Again, the key is to keep the house as close to the flowers as possible.

Schedule of Materials: Butterfly House

LTR.	NO.	ITEM	STOCK	INCHES T	(MM) T	INCHES W	(MM) W	INCHES L	(MM) L	COMMENTS
A	1	front	pine	½	(13)	5½	(140)	15	(381)	
B	2	sides	pine	½	(13)	3½	(89)	15	(381)	
C	1	back	pine	½	(13)	5½	(140)	15	(381)	
D	1	roof	pine	½	(13)	5½	(140)	7	(178)	
E	1	floor	pine	½	(13)	5	(127)	6¼	(159)	
F	n/a	roost	bark/branch							cut to fit; any natural material with bark is fine

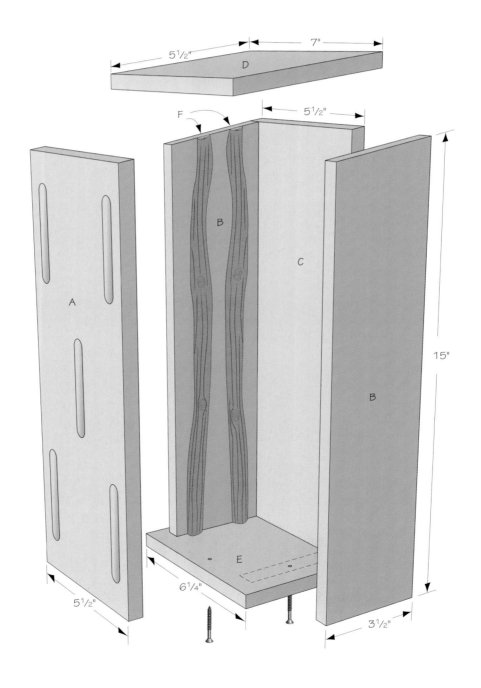

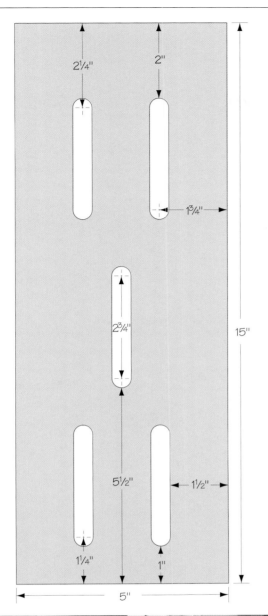

2¼"

2"

1¾"

2¾"

5½"

1½"

1¼"

1"

15"

5"

FIGURE 1 Drill two ½"-diameter holes spaced 2¾" on center. Connect the holes with lines and make the cuts.

FIGURE 2 Bark or branches covered in bark make great perches for the butterflies.

FIGURE 3 Assemble the entire box, then cut the 10° top slope on the whole thing at one time using your band saw.

FIGURE 4 Attach the roof with four screws.

Traditional Bluebird Box

BY A. J. HAMLER

Bluebirds are among the most-loved species in America, and for good reason: They're attractive, have a beautiful song, and earn their keep by eating lots of pesky insects.

Organizations devoted to the bluebird are among the largest of all bird devotees, and when traveling around the country you're likely to see more bluebird houses along the roadsides than any other type.

While the newer design of the Peterson Bluebird Box in the next the chapter has proven very successful, bluebirds still love the more-familiar, standard square box that has been around for many years. By changing dimensions and other attributes, this basic design can be used as the basis for houses intended for many other species. In fact, the Swallow House project elsewhere in this book is of a similar design.

For this project, I've used guidelines from the North American Bluebird Society (NABS) (www.nabluebirdsociety.org) as my starting point, but made some changes to create a sturdier house. The house is made entirely of ¾" cedar.

Cut the house sides, top and floor to size, then cut ¼" – ⅜" off each corner of the floor as shown in the drawing for drainage/ventilation. Also go ahead and cut the front and back to length, but don't cut them to width yet. The sides, one of which will act as a lift-up door to access the interior, are angled at the top

to match the roof slope of 10°, so a miter saw is the perfect tool to use when cutting the sides to length. (Fig. 1) You can also use a handsaw, or a table saw with a miter gauge, to make these cuts.

Now, why did I recommend waiting to cut the front and back to width? Off-the-shelf cedar—even though sold as ¾" thick—is often a bit thicker. That was the case with the stock I purchased for this house project; in fact, the ¾" cedar I got was ⅞", a full ⅛" thicker than its nominal thickness. Because this extra size can throw off dimensions, I opted to dry-assemble the house to check its exact width before cutting the front and back to width. Good thing I did, as the thicker sides extended the width of the front and back by ¼" beyond the 5½" listed in the cut list for this project. As a result, you should always check the thickness of your stock – especially cedar – when sizing your components.

One easy way to make the adjustment is shown in Fig. 2. With my table saw unplugged, I've dry-assembled the floor and sides right against the blade, and then moved the fence in and locked it down. (Note the 5¾" adjusted width indicated by my steel rule.) Because the fence setting now matches the house

width, when I cut the front and back to size, they'll be a perfect fit.

Both the front, back and roof are beveled to match the 10° roof slope, which I've elected to do on the table saw in Fig. 3. The front and back is beveled at the top, while the roof is beveled at the back. When cutting the bevel on the front, be sure to orient the bevel such that the rough side of the wood faces inward.

Drill a 1½" entrance hole through the front 6½" up from the bottom edge, as in Fig 4. The Forstner bit I'm using in Fig. 4 makes a very clean hole, but you can also use a hole saw. Place a piece of scrap beneath the workpiece to prevent tear-out on the back side. For safety, note that I've clamped the workpiece to the drill press table. In addition to the traditional round hole we're using here, bluebirds will also accept a 1⅜" × 2¼" oval hole, which I'll describe for the Peterson Bluebird Box in the next chapter. You can use either type for bluebird houses.

Using glue and nails, assemble the back, right side, front and floor, making sure that the beveled front and back align with the angled left side. The reason I've suggested to orient the front with the rough side in is to give nestlings an easier surface to climb when it's time to leave the nest. The cedar I used for this house was very rough, and it will work fine for the nestlings. However, if the cedar you get is particularly smooth on both sides, you may need to add some shallow cuts the nestlings can grab onto. I'll describe this alternative method in the next chapter.

Now, test-fit the left-side door,

Schedule of Materials: Traditional Bluebird Box

LTR.	NO.	ITEM	STOCK	INCHES T	(MM) T	INCHES W	(MM) W	INCHES L	(MM) L	COMMENTS
A	1	back	cedar	¾	(19)	5½	(140)	14½	(368)	Length of back adjusted as needed for mounting.
B	1	front	cedar	¾	(19)	5½	(140)	9⅜	(238)	
C	1	left side	cedar	¾	(19)	5½	(140)	10	(254)	
D	1	right side	cedar	¾	(19)	5½	(140)	10¼	(260)	
E	1	floor	cedar	¾	(19)	5½	(140)	4	(102)	
F	1	roof	cedar	¾	(19)	8	(203)	10	(254)	

adjusting it with sandpaper or hand plane if it's too tight so that it will pivot easily. The left side is shorter than the right, and will leave a ¼" ventilation gap at the top. With the bottom edge of the door even with the bottom of the house, measure about 7½" up from the floor of the house and drive a galvanized nail through both the front and back of the house to act as hinges. (Fig. 5) Measure the nail locations exactly the same front and back so the door pivots properly. Drill a small hole 1" to 2" up from the bottom of the house and into the door edge and slip in a galvanized nail that will act as a lock to keep the door closed. Depending on how you plan to mount your house, you can drill this lock hole through either the front or back.

Finally, run a bead of glue along all the top edges, except the door, and nail the roof in place so the rear bevel is flush with the back.

The original NABS specifications for this house called for ventilation gaps on both sides of the house. However, that meant that the roof would be anchored on only the front and back of the house. I increased the height of the right side so it was flush with the underside of the roof, providing an additional attachment edge. Between the ventilation gap above the door, the entrance hole and the notches in the corners of the floor, this design offers plenty of fresh air circulation.

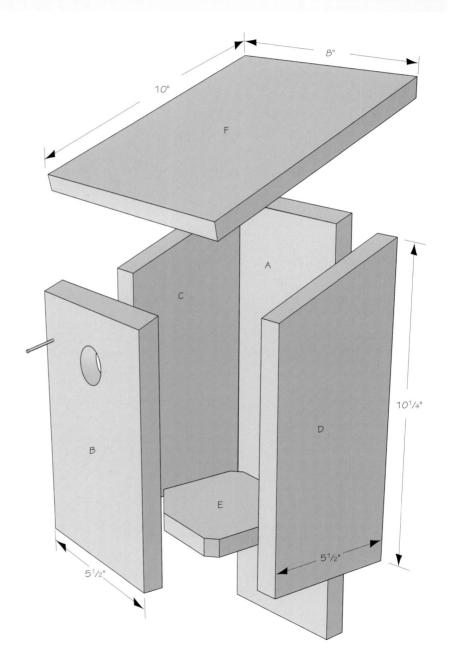

FIGURE 1 Either a miter saw, a handsaw or a table saw with a miter gauge can be used to cut the miters on the parts.

FIGURE 2 Here's an easy way to adjust the fence on your table saw for cutting the front and back parts to width.

FIGURE 3 The bevels on the top edges of the front, back and back of the top can be easily cut on the table saw.

FIGURE 4 A Forstner bit cuts a clean hole with smooth edges. You could also cut the hole using a hole saw.

FIGURE 5 Make sure the nails are the same distance from the bottom of the box so they function properly as hinges.

Cottage Birdhouse

BY A. J. HAMLER

Everyone loves a cozy cottage, even our feathered friends. This cottage is ideal for any bird from tiny wrens up to house finches—just adjust the size of the entrance hole.

Smaller birds will find the house roomier than they're used to, but they'll adjust quickly.

Since this cottage is modeled after the Finch House, you'll find that many of the components are similar to those for that project, with some even being the same size. However, where the Finch House was made entirely with ¾" cedar, this one uses a mix of materials from ½" plywood to ⅛"-thick plywood trim for windows and doors. I've taken decorating this house to the extreme by adding thin clapboard siding and cedar shingles, but feel free to do without those touches for a simpler, faster project by just skipping over those steps.

Lay out cutlines for the components on your stock as in Fig. 1. After marking, I cut this workpiece in half right through the center of the "X", then attached the two pieces together to cut the roof angles on both pieces at the same time. (I've done that throughout this book for identical pieces.) As with the Finch House, this one also has a 90° crown, so the house sides are beveled at 45° on their top edges, while the front and back components are cut to a tapered point at 45° angles on each side. When you have the front and back completed, cut ½" off

the pointed top of the back workpiece for a ventilation opening.

Unlike the Bluebird House, the cottage does not have a pivoting side for access (access here will be through the removable base). So, start assembly by attaching the front and back of the house to the two sides with waterproof glue and nails, as shown in Fig. 2.

If you're adding siding, measure and mark it to fit as in Fig. 3. With a piece of scrap underneath, use a sharp utility knife (or a fine-cut saw) to cut your siding to size.

Before attaching the siding, glue and clamp a hardwood disc of the appropriate size for your intended occupants about 6" up the front of the house; the process here is the same as for the Lighthouse in an earlier chapter. This cottage is for wrens—one of my favorites—so I used a 1¾" disc and drilled a 1⅛" hole through its center. But again, the 5½" × 6½" floor of this house can accommodate a wide range of birds so use a disc of whatever size you prefer and drill the appropriate hole.

Start the siding on the back of the house. Spread a thin layer of glue over the area where the first piece of siding will go as in Fig. 5. Press the siding into

place. Place a piece of scrap large enough to cover the siding and clamp in place around the edges until dry. Attaching siding can be a slow process, as you need to wait for the glue to set before moving on to the next piece. I've found that because the glue is spread in such thin layers, you can usually unclamp and move to the next piece after about 20-25 minutes. When the first piece is dry, spread more glue on the next section and press the next piece of siding in place, butting it up against the first. Clamp as before. Move on up the back of the house, and trim off the overhang at the edges of the roof line.

Although you could add windows and doors right on top of the clapboard siding, because the siding is channeled there's always an opportunity for water to get underneath. For that reason I've opted to add my doors and windows first, and fit the siding around them. This involves a lot of cutting and fitting, but the effort is worth it, and the process of priming and painting will do a great job of sealing all edges. I've created my own windows here using ⅛" plywood, as you can see in Fig. 6. However, you can find a huge variety of ready-made (and quite fancy) doors and windows through any dollhouse supplier.

Glue your door and windows in place, and then it's just a matter of cutting and fitting smaller pieces of siding around them as in Fig. 7. Work your way up the sides and front of the house. In Fig. 8, you can see how I've cut the siding to fit around the entrance ring. I used a spare hardwood disc to first trace

the circular outline on the siding, and then cut it out with a sharp utility knife. Note in this photo that I didn't put siding between the windows and doors; instead, I'll put shutters there—it's a lot easier than cutting thin strips of siding and getting the clapboard aligned correctly.

Starting with the narrower roof side, apply glue to the angled edges of the side, front and back, then align the roof carefully and nail it into place. Do the same on the other side and nail that half of the roof in place.

Although it's a bit time-consuming,

Schedule of Materials: Cottage

LTR.	NO.	ITEM	STOCK	INCHES T	(MM) T	INCHES W	(MM) W	INCHES L	(MM) L
A	2	front/back	plywood	½	(13)	6½	(165)	8¼	(209)
B	2	sides	plywood	½	(13)	5½	(140)	6½	(165)
C	1	left roof	plywood	½	(13)	5¼	(133)	9¾	(248)
D	1	right roof	plywood	½	(13)	5¾	(146)	9¾	(248)
E	1	bottom	pine	¾	(19)	7¼	(184)	8¾	(402)
F	1	entrance ring	hardwood disc	³⁄₁₆	(5)	1¾ d	(45)		

All windows and doors constructed of ⅛" plywood. Roof crown trim strips are ⅛" cedar. Basswood clapboard siding and cedar shingles are available through dollhouse suppliers.

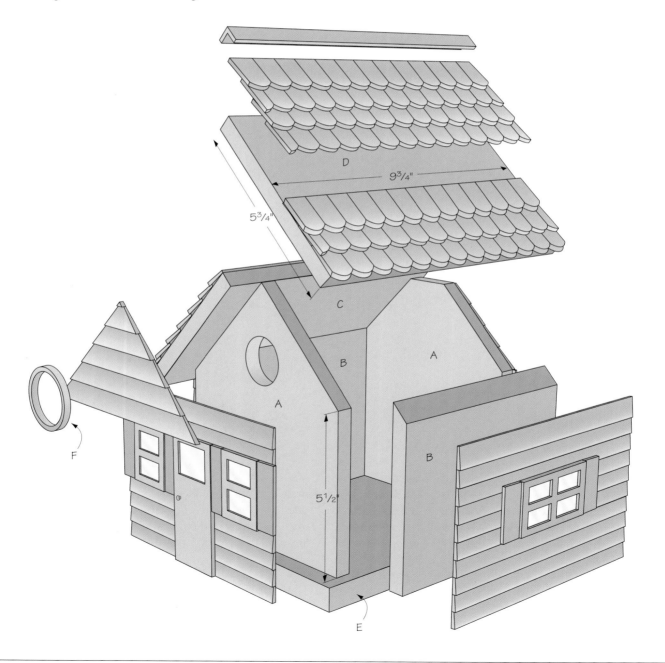

applying cedar shingles—available from any dollhouse supplier—is very easy. First, seal the roof of the house thoroughly with a good primer. Then, mark parallel lines down each side of the roof at a distance determined by the length of the shingles. The shingles you get may recommend a specific overlap of each row, but overlapping ⅜" is about right for most. You can use regular woodworking glue to attach shingles, but if you ever need to repair the roof, removing damaged shingles is a real pain. For that reason, I opted for hot-melt glue, which not only makes the job of hanging shingles much faster, it's far easier to remove a damaged shingle and replace it. (Fig. 9) The last step for the roof after attaching shingles is to add a pair of ⅛"-thick cedar trim strips on either side of the roof crown.

Now it's just a matter of priming and painting the house any way you prefer, then adding the shutters and whatever trim you'd like, such as the doorknob you see in the final photo. You can find all manner of trim at a dollhouse supplier: brass doorknobs and mail slots, porch lights, weathervanes, you name it.

Finally, mount the cottage to the base by driving four screws up through the bottom and into the assembly. A few ¼" or ⅜" holes drilled through the base provide drainage.

There are endless variations you can make to this birdhouse—size, structure, colors, trim and more. Because I've designed this house with a roof that overhangs on all four sides, it's best mounted on a pole using one of the methods described in Part One of this book. If you'd prefer to mount it flush on a tree trunk, alter the construction so that the roof and base do not overhang in the back.

As I mentioned earlier, you don't have to go through all the effort to add the siding and roofing shingles, which admittedly takes a long time. This cottage house would look just as nice with a simple, attractive paint job. But if you do go the extra mile, you've not only created an attractive birdhouse. You may have created an heirloom.

FIGURE 1 Lay out the cutlines for the front/back parts

FIGURE 2 Start assembly by attaching the front and back of the house to the two sides with waterproof glue and nails.

FIGURE 3 If you're adding siding, now is the time to do it.

FIGURE 4 With a piece of scrap underneath, use a sharp utility knife (or a fine-cut saw) to cut your siding to size.

FIGURE 5 Spread a thin layer of glue over the area where the first piece of siding will go.

FIGURE 6 I used ⅛" plywood to make my windows and door.

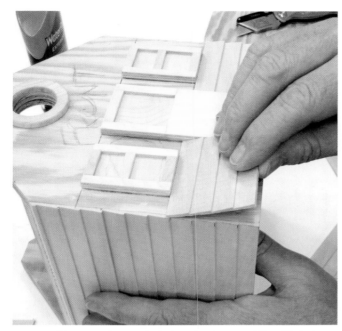

FIGURE 7 Glue your door and windows in place, and then it's just a matter of cutting and fitting smaller pieces of siding around them.

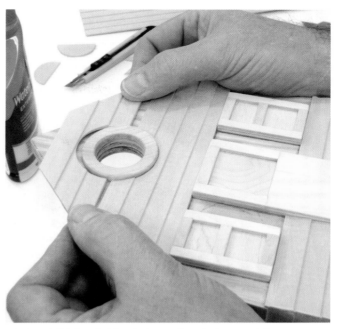

FIGURE 8 I didn't put siding between the windows and doors; instead, I'll put shutters there.

FIGURE 9 I opted for hot-melt glue, which not only makes the job of hanging shingles much faster, it's far easier to remove a damaged shingle and replace it.

Outdoor Lantern

BY CHRISTOPHER SCHWARZ

Add some mood lighting to your next outdoor affair with this great Arts & Crafts luminary.

Call me dull, but I've never been a Tiki torch kind of guy. And the last time we lit an outdoor party we used oil lamps—which, because of the flammable nature of oil, almost ended in disaster. So my task before our next party was to build a lantern that's low-key and electric (to ensure that only ribs were barbecued and not the neighbor's dog).

This lamp can be used in a variety of ways. It looks great on a patio table, or you could glue 6"-long dowels into the feet and stake it in your garden. Either way, it's going to stand up to the elements.

The lantern's body is made from quartersawn white-oak scraps. The "rice paper" behind the slats is actually acrylic ($4 for an 18" x 24" sheet) that I sanded on both sides with a random-orbit sander and installed in the lantern using waterproof silicone.

The light fixture itself ($3 from my nearby home center) is vinyl clad and is intended for outdoor use. It's also installed in the base of the lamp using silicone.

Construction

There's no complicated joinery in this project, but it does require more preci-

sion and care than most outdoor furniture. Essentially, the four panels are glued at the edges to the four posts. This is a long-grain-to-long-grain joint, so no real joinery is required. However, to keep all the parts aligned during glue-up, I used a single No. 10 biscuit in each joint. This saved me some real headaches when clamping.

The lamp base, which holds the light fixture, rests on two cleats nailed to the inside of the panels. The removable top is held in position by four cleats nailed to the underside of the top.

Begin construction by cutting out all your parts. Cutting the five ⅜"-wide slots in the panels—the first task—is the trickiest part of the whole project. Once you do that, you can breathe easier.

There are several ways to cut these

slots. A plunge router with an edge guide is an obvious way to go about it. I chose to use a dado stack in my table saw. Place a dado stack measuring ⅜" wide into your table saw and get out your miter gauge or table saw sled, which will hold the work during the cut. You'll make a plunge cut into the panel for each slot.

First pencil a line on both long edges of the panel that shows where the slot should start and end. Position your panel slightly back of the blade's center, then raise the blade until it emerges from the panel and has nibbled to the far line. Move the piece forward until the dado stack nibbles to the near line. Lower the dado stack back under the saw's table, move the workpiece over ¾" and repeat the same process.

Make sure you hold or clamp the stock firmly against your miter gauge's fence as you raise the dado stack. If you let the workpiece shift, it's very likely that it will self-destruct in your hands.

If you're feeling like these slots are more work then they're worth, consider other patterns. You can drill a series of holes with a drill press, or you can use a scroll saw to create a design that suits your brand of outdoor parties.

After all of your panels are cut, sand them to their finished grit or take a hand plane to them before turning your attention to milling the four posts.

Five-sided Posts

As I mentioned earlier, I used a biscuit in each joint to line everything up during assembly. Now it's time to cut those biscuit slots. Mark the location of each slot and cut a recess for a No. 10 biscuit in each post and in each long edge of the panels.

You could leave the posts square and your lantern will look fine. I tapered one corner to give the lantern a lighter look. The taper clips ⅜" off the top outside corner of each post and then tapers to nothing at the base.

Some woodworkers might build a jig to make this cut. The simplest way is to mark the taper in pencil on the post, then plane down to that line using a block plane or bench plane. Each post should take less than five minutes to complete.

Sand your posts to their final grit and you're ready for assembly.

Assembly

Don't try to glue up all four posts at once. You'll want to be able to adjust the panels and posts as you clamp everything, and eight parts sliding around is enough to make any woodworker panic.

When deciding which posts should go where, take a look at the figure. Each post should have one face that is flat-sawn grain and one that is quartersawn grain. Position the posts so the flat-sawn grain faces are together and the quartersawn grain faces are together. This is one of those things that might bug you about a project years later.

Begin by gluing up two assemblies that have two posts and one panel. While the glue is drying, nail the cleats for the lamp base to the other two panels in the location shown in the illustration at right. Then glue the two assemblies to the two remaining panels.

Final Details

Next, turn your attention to the top. Begin by cutting the ⅜" x ⅜" chamfer on the underside of all four edges. To let the heat from the light bulb escape, drill four ⅜"-diameter holes in the top, following the diagram.

Glue and nail the spacers to the top. Then add the top caps on top of the spacers. Screw and glue the feet centered on the posts.

The light fixture I purchased for this lantern was

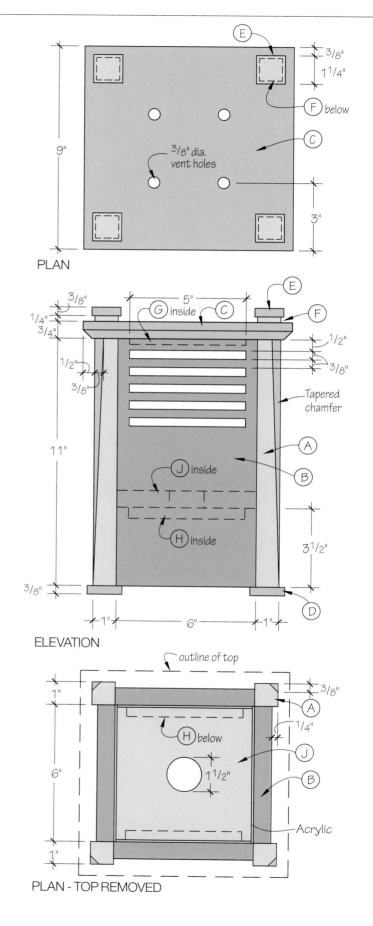

PLAN

ELEVATION

PLAN - TOP REMOVED

Schedule of Materials: Outdoor Lantern

NO.	LTR.	ITEM	DIMENSIONS (INCHES)		
			T	W	L
4	A	Posts	1	1	11
4	B	Panels	¾	6	11
1	C	Top	¾	9	9
4	D	Feet	³⁄₈	1½	1½
4	E	Top caps	³⁄₈	1¼	1¼
4	F	Spacers	¼	1	1
4	G	Cleats to hold top	¼	¼	5
2	H	Cleats to hold lamp base	½		

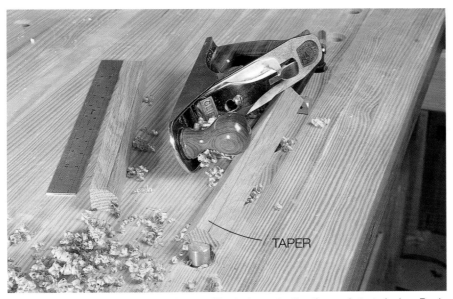

TAPER

Clamp the post with one corner facing up. Check the grain direction and start planing. Begin with short strokes at the top of the post and, as your taper lengthens, make your strokes longer.

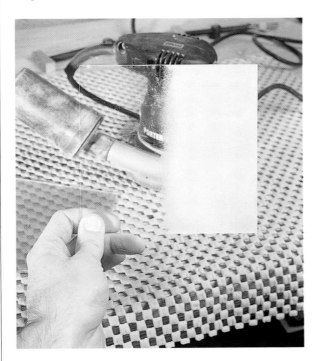

Load your sander with #100-grit sandpaper and sand both sides of the acrylic. It takes only a couple of minutes to turn the clear plastic into frosted plastic.

designed to sit in a 1½"-diameter hole. Drill the hole for your fixture in the center of the lamp base and attach the fixture to the base using silicone. Then attach the lamp base to the cleats using (again) a little dab of silicone.

The "rice paper" is my favorite part of the project. It's made from inexpensive ³⁄₃₂"-thick acrylic I bought at my local hardware store in the glass section. Cut the acrylic to size using your table saw and sand both faces with a random-orbit sander to get a frosted effect. Attach acrylic to the inside face of each panel using silicone. A spring clamp will hold it in place while the silicone cures.

Four cleats hold the top in position on the base. Turn the entire lamp upside down on your bench with the base centered on the underside of the top. Mark the location of the base. Measure in from those lines the combined thickness of the panels and the acrylic. Then nail four cleats at those locations.

As for the finish, I left mine natural for now. I might someday put a few coats of an outdoor finish on it, such as tung oil. But first I want to see if it survives our next outdoor party.

Folding Plant Stand

BY JIM STUARD

Less than one sheet of plywood and a long afternoon are all you need to build a functional and foldable floral display.

When you have a lot of plants to display, you are always looking for ways to show them off to their best advantage. Or maybe you just want to cover that hole where a gopher dug under the house. Either way this plant stand is a great way to make a few potted plants look like a huge display. And here's a bonus feature: the whole thing folds up flat so you can hang it on a garage wall in the off-season. You can make it using about three-quarters of a sheet of ¾" CDX plywood, which is essential for outdoor use. The term CDX refers to the quality of the two face veneers and the glue between the plys. So CDX has a "C" and a "D" side ("A" being the best grade) with the "X" referring to the exterior-grade glue. The plys themselves are the same as in any other pine plywood. The shelves are designed to hold 6" pots, but with care, larger pots are also okay.

Start with two four-foot square sheets of plywood, and begin construction by cutting out the back and supports from one sheet and the shelves from the other. Use the diagrams to lay out your cuts. To cut the shelves and supports from the ply, use a drill with a ³⁄₁₆" bit to drill two overlapping holes for the jigsaw blade. Drill clearance holes at the outside cor-

ners of the back and supports to start the saw blade. If you clamp the parts to a table, you can cut the shapes in short order. Once you get the back and supports cut, you'll notice that the steps on the support are ¾" shorter than the back. This helps everything fold flat for storage.

The next step is to cut ¾" x 4" notches in the tops of the steps, at the back, to receive the hinge mounting blocks for the shelves. Use screws and water resistant glue to attach the mounting blocks. When installed, the blocks stick out 1" from the edge of the back and ¾" from the surface. These locations line up with the shelves and give an offset to clear the supports when everything is folded. Adjust the fit until the supports fit into the notches on the back, then mount the supports to the back. Take four butt hinges and place them where they will be mounted. Mark the locations with a pencil and then take the supports off the back. You need to rout a recess in the support and the back for the hinge. Otherwise, there won't be enough clearance for the shelves to come down. Mount the hinges and check the fit of the supports to make sure they clear the mounting blocks. At this time, go ahead

and paint the back/support assembly. This is easier now than when everything is assembled. Also fill any voids and knots with a waterproof filler. I used a two-part auto body filler. It sets up quickly and sands easily.

The last thing to do is cut and mount the shelves. Begin the layout with a set of trammel points, with a pencil on one end. From the center of the other plywood panel, lay out concentric semi-circles at 5", 10", 15" and 20". Now rip the panel at about 21" to keep it manageable. Cut the shelves out using a jigsaw, taking it slow and stay on the line. When you're done, you'll have four concentric shelves ready for mounting. After filling the voids and knots, paint the shelves. Lay out and rout a recess on the bottom of the shelf ends to accept the hinge leaf, flush to the shelf. This also helps for the close tolerances when folding everything together. Go ahead and mount the shelves to the back. When you're all done, lay the unit on its back and fold the shelves so they're sticking straight up. Fold up the supports and tip the entire unit upright. Touch up any paint problems and you're ready to lush up this display with the local flora.

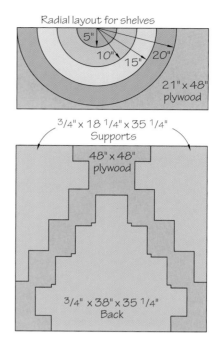

Radial layout for shelves

5"

10" 15" 20"

21" x 48" plywood

3/4" x 18 1/4" x 35 1/4" Supports

48" x 48" plywood

3/4" x 38" x 35 1/4" Back

To set up the plant stand, lay it flat on its back and raise the shelves. Then fold the supports up.

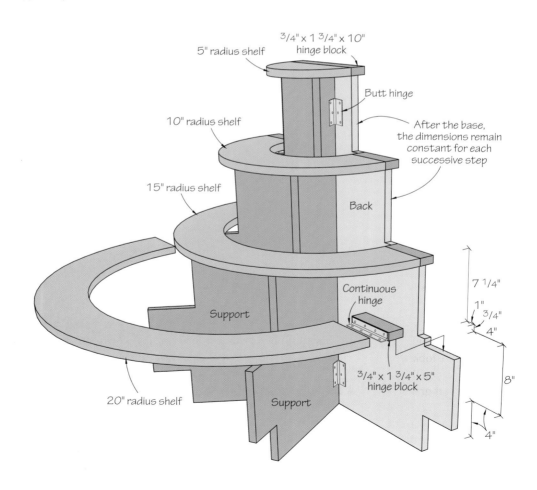

3/4" x 1 3/4" x 10" hinge block

5" radius shelf

Butt hinge

After the base, the dimensions remain constant for each successive step

10" radius shelf

15" radius shelf

Back

Continuous hinge

Support

7 1/4"

1"

3/4"

4"

3/4" x 1 3/4" x 5" hinge block

8"

Support

20" radius shelf

4"

Build a Boomerang

BY TREVOR SMITH

Making a boomerang is simple, fast and will set your head spinning. Boomerangs come in a surprising number of shapes. All of these versions fly.

ABOUT TO TAKE FLIGHT. The students loved watching their classmates throw boomerangs almost as much as they enjoyed throwing them. Above, Jon Roberts throws his "Bat-erang" as his friends observe his effortless (athletic) throwing technique from a safe distance behind.From the look on Jon's face it is easy to see that Troy High School students take boomerangs very seriously.

If you like a challenge, enjoy having an excuse to be outside and are looking for ideas for practical projects, you'll find that building a boomerang is great fun.

Also, boomerangs are a great project to build with family members you've wanted to introduce to woodworking. And when you are done you get to go to the park and spend time together throwing them.

I have just one warning: Boomerangs will draw a curious crowd of onlookers.

A Little Science of Boomerangs

Here's the first rule of boomerangs: Do not be afraid of trial and error. There are a wide variety of shapes that will work.

Boomerangs operate on the principle of "gyroscopic precession," which is similar to riding a bike no handed and

attempting to initiate a turn. In bike riding, the spinning (gyroscopic) motion of the wheels gives the bike stability. To execute a "no hands" bicycle turn, you simply lean the bike in the direction that you wish to turn. The wheels have a delayed reaction to the force of the leaning action. This way, the wheels actually feel the force a quarter turn from where the force was applied. So instead of fall-

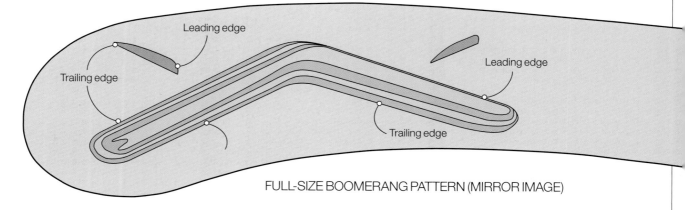

Leading edge

Trailing edge

Leading edge

Trailing edge

FULL-SIZE BOOMERANG PATTERN (MIRROR IMAGE)

ing over, the bicycle turns in the desired direction.

Unlike riding a bicycle with "no hands" while turning, the boomerang experiences a continuous turn as the force is applied for the duration of the flight. The boomerang is thrown with a slight tilt from vertical (more on this later). The gyroscopic nature of a spinning boomerang and the release angle (called the "layover angle") causes the boomerang's flight angle to flatten out as it turns. Thus a well-balanced, well-contoured and well-thrown boomerang will return to the thrower in a horizontal hover. Most people expect that this will take practice though.

The duration of flight is determined by the force with which the boomerang was thrown as well as the spin applied at launch. As with any object flying through the air, a boomerang is subject to drag its own weight as it makes its flight pattern. This drag slows the boomerang down, thereby limiting the flight time. However, given enough spin and initial velocity, the boomerang will circle above the thrower's head a few times before landing.

Choosing a Shape And a Material

Even if you don't fully understand how boomerangs work, you can still make one that flies quite well. There are a wide variety of plans available on the Internet (type in "boomerang plans" into any search engine). Or you can start with the scaled plans here or download full plans

from the *Popular Woodworking* web site that you can print and adhere directly to the wood.

For your first boomerang, pick a simple design, which will be easy to make and throw. In other words, it is best not to pick a complex design that is for trick flying.

The traditional wood used by the aboriginal tribes of Australia to make boomerangs is Myall brigalow (*Acacia harpophylla*). According to George Simonds Boulger in his book "Wood: A Manual of the Natural History and Industrial Applications of the Timber of Commerce" (BiblioLife), this native wood is "brown, strongly violet-scented, very heavy, very hard, elastic, durable, splitting freely. Used for turnery, tobacco-pipes, vine-stakes, spears and boomerangs."

A practical, quality and easy-to-work-with material for this project is plywood. However, the plywood at the big box stores isn't a good choice. Boomerangs are essentially flying wings, and better grades of plywood are more durable. In fact some plywoods are engineered for flying projects.

When I teach high school physics students to build boomerangs, I prefer to use ¼"-thick Baltic birch or Finnish birch. Baltic birch costs less, but Finnish birch is laminated with waterproof glue so it can hold up better outdoors. The two plywoods are easy to tell apart. The glue lines for Baltic are similar in color to the wood. The waterproof glue used in Finnish birch is a dark chocolate color.

Rough Out Your Boomerang

Once you have your wood and a pattern, you'll need to gather the tools. You need some sort of saw that can cut curves, such as a band saw, coping saw or bowsaw. To smooth the shape and thin the edges of your boomerang you need files and sandpaper. A spindle sander is nice to have, but it is not required.

If you are going to make several boomerangs in one shape, I recommend you make a pattern. We use paper bags, poster board or thin plastic sheeting.

Transfer the boomerang's shape to the wood blank. Then cut the shape out with your saw. I use this opportunity to teach the physics students how to use a band saw safely. Many students have never used power tools and this was a great way to introduce their safe use.

I survey my students about their experiences with the tools, and here's what one female student, Lo Struga, had to say about the band saw: "It felt like the first time I heard the Beatles, it was amazing."

Once the shape of the boomerang is sawn out, you can refine its outline with a spindle sander or files and sandpaper.

Shaping the Airfoil

Now you need to make some important decisions. Like golf clubs, boomerangs are "handed." How the boomerang's airfoil is laid out and shaped depends on whether the person who is going to throw the boomerang is right-handed or left-handed.

The illustration above shows the air-

ILLUSTRATIONS BY ROBERT W. LANG

HERE'S THE WINDUP. "Beast" was one mean flying wing. Demonstrating that not only do you have to have a carefully made boomerang for success, but also good throwing form, Do H. Kim throws the boomerang he made. Notice the pinch grip as Do Kim prepares to release his boomerang into flight. Everyone would stop to watch when "Beast" was launched; it flew that well.

foil shape of a right-handed boomerang. For a left-handed boomerang, you simply reverse the airfoil shape.

First mark the top of the boomerang. As with airplane wings, the airfoils on a boomerang have a leading and a trailing edge. The leading edge is a quarter-round shape and the trailing edge tapers off the top of the boomerang like the cross-section of a typical airplane wing. Mark the two leading edges and the two trailing edges so you do not file them incorrectly (a common mistake my students make). The bottom face of the wing is completely flat.

Lay out the leading and trailing edges of the wings based on which hand will do the throwing. A marking gauge can be used for this (or the old trick of holding a finger against the edge). Mark in on the top the distance that the contour retreats back from the boomerang's edge to its top surface.

The quarter-round shape generally extends about ¼" from the edge, while the trailing edge extends about 1" to 1½" into the material. Note that you only have to shape one face of the plywood. The other face is left flat. See the illustration below to understand how the airfoil shape looks on a simple "V"-shaped boomerang. Note how the leading edge and trailing edge change along the length of the boomerang.

Shape the airfoil with rasps, files and sandpaper. There are a variety of rasps available out there. We use Nicholson cabinetmakers No. 49 and 50 cabinet

START WITH A SIMPLE PATTERN. Melanie Jonas traces a bi-wing pattern onto ¼" plywood. The next step is to head over to the band saw. This pattern was so popular that I made a wooden pattern for the students to be able to trace.

SWOOPING CUTS. There are two large Powermatic band saws in the school shop. Our Industrial Technology teacher, Al Merian, was a great help, generously making the shop available to the physics students. Here Danny Forche is cutting out his boomerang while a line of students wait their turns at the band saw. Just like woodworking school.

rasps. These tools fascinated the students and they understood their importance to the whole process.

"The files (and rasps) were indeed important in the success of our boomerangs because the files sculpted the airfoils," Drew Jarvis commented.

And Whitney Regalski added: "Without files, the shape I was shooting for would never have been accomplished."

A boomerang is actually a flying rotating rotor, like on a helicopter. The airfoil shape needs to be consistent, and this is where the plys in plywood help in the design of the project. As the glue lines appear from the plys it is easy to observe the progress when shaping of the airfoils.

The optional finishing touch to shaping the airfoil is to slightly bevel the back edge of the wing (if you wish). Or, another option is to make some test

SMOOTH EDGES SOAR. At the spindle sander, Todd Geiser refines the edge of his boomerang blank. The spindle sander is an efficient tool for smoothing the perimeter of the boomerang. Getting one smooth and fair line all the way around the boomerang is the goal at this stage.

RASP YOUR AIRFOIL. Clamps help to steady the boomerang blank while the airfoil is brought to life. In this photo, Mike Laba uses a rasp to make quick work of the shaping process. Notice that Mike has positioned the boomerang off the edge of the bench so the the rasp does not damage Mr. Merian's benches.

FINE-TUNE WITH SANDPAPER. After a couple test flights, Andrew Mihoc adds some refinement to the shape of the airfoils on this tri-blade boomerang with some sandpaper.

throws first and see if your boomerang is making a complete turn. If it is not, then file a slight back bevel on the flat face of the leading edge.

Before you decorate your boomerang, you should take it for a test spin because you might want to refine its airfoil.

Throwing Technique
When teaching students to throw a boomerang, we start by using example boomerangs made with paper and cardboard in the classroom.

Throwing requires a little practice, so it is worth the time to make a few quick cardboard practice boomerangs. Cereal boxes are a great raw material for this. You can make a quick cardboard boomerang using two strips of cardboard approximately 1" wide and 8" to 10" long. Use hot-melt glue to form them into the shape of a plus sign. Put a gentle upward curl on the four blades and throw using the same techniques described below for throwing wooden boomerangs.

The throwing technique has a few

key components, regardless of the material. Pinch the boomerang between your thumb and index finger and hold it over your head. Your thumb grasps the airfoil shape. The index finger is against the flat face of the boomerang.

Now hold your arm perfectly vertical. Before you throw, you need to tilt your arm 10° to 20° away from your body. This is called the "layover angle." See the illustration on the next page for what this looks like.

The throwing motion employs a lot of wrist action to generate the necessary spin around the center of mass of the thrown wing. Throw the boomerang at an angle of 45° from the front of the body. (That's with straight out in front being 0° and arms held straight out at the sides being 90°.) The angles are guidelines to get you started in the right direction. Do not be afraid to experiment with the throwing angles.

When throwing a boomerang outside, the wind should be light and blowing straight into your face. The throw is still 45° from the front. Aim for a point about 10° above the horizon. This will send the boomerang flying. See the illustrations on the next page for details.

One of the important reasons to make indoor boomerangs before making wood ones is to learn the throwing

motion. Indoors, the flight patterns are smaller, and the feedback for good and poor throws and working designs occurs quickly. The cardboard 'rangs are quite harmless if they hit someone, too.

Once everyone is able to prove that they can throw a boomerang and not a "stick" or "kylie" (as a non-returning boomerang is called in Australia), then it is time to find a place outside to throw your wooden version.

Find a Space to Throw
The larger the throwing area the better, especially when learning to throw. Parks are areas worth scouting. A football or soccer field is a good-size space to start with. There is less chance of losing a boomerang if the area is very large. Do not throw in an area where there are children, pets, cars or structures that may get in the way.

After five years of teaching physics students to make and throw boomerangs, there have been a few surprises. One surprise is just how well the boomerangs fly. The other shock is just how much the students enjoy the entire process. They carry their boomerangs around the school and even trade boomerangs with one another.

And a few times every year some students will bring some boomerangs to class that they didn't make at school. Yup. The students have been at home making boomerangs with their parents. One female student said that she didn't have any interest in her dad's shop until they made a boomerang together. In several cases, the student's parents became so interested in the boomerangs that once the kids showed their parents (and even grandparents) how to make them, they would make boomerangs on their own.

PERFECT FORM. Just as it begins to rain, J.D. Dennison cannot resist one last throw of a tri-wing boomerang. Tri-wing boomerangs spin very fast, but do not fly as far as the more traditional bi-wings. It is easy to see from Dennison's wind-up that boomerangs can be thrown quite hard.

How to Throw a Boomerang

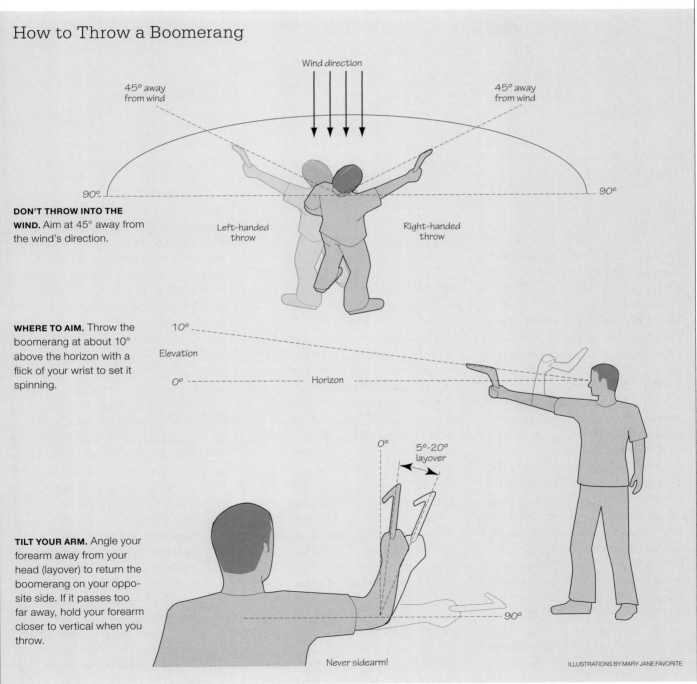

DON'T THROW INTO THE WIND. Aim at 45° away from the wind's direction.

WHERE TO AIM. Throw the boomerang at about 10° above the horizon with a flick of your wrist to set it spinning.

TILT YOUR ARM. Angle your forearm away from your head (layover) to return the boomerang on your opposite side. If it passes too far away, hold your forearm closer to vertical when you throw.

ILLUSTRATIONS BY MARY JANE FAVORITE

Canoe Paddle

BY JOHN WILSON

A single length of framing lumber will help you hone your skills with a spokeshave, a drawknife and a block plane.

It was a bright summer's day in 1993 at historic Strawbery Banke in Portsmouth, N.H. My wife, Sally, and I were unexpectedly in town and noticed a craft show and demonstrations on the green. The area is famous for such crafts as coopering and building Windsor chairs and wooden boats. I've always been fascinated to watch skilled demonstrators, and this demonstration by boatbuilder Geoff Burke would not be a disappointment.

Burke captivated onlookers while he made a canoe paddle. Here was a familiar object being made with a few hand tools. The material was a straight-grained 2x6 plank of spruce commonly used for residential framing. The time it took him to carve the paddle: less than one hour.

Everyone appreciated the efficiency with which the job was accomplished (not that reducing the blade thickness with a drawknife is easy—it's not). But the key is choosing the right tool for each step of the project, knowing how to put the right tool to use and having an eye for proportion to guide it.

But you should be forewarned. A paddle is sculpture in a traditional form and requires a practiced eye for proportion. This is something we're all born

with to a degree, and we can develop it with practice. The exact ratio of "birth-given" and "practice-acquired" is a mystery. I have observed a wide range of accomplishment among my boatbuilding students when assigned this task. Most of my students made a functional paddle; few were able to make a graceful one their first time.

Today, paddle blanks stand in a corner of my shop, some cut out, some waiting as a piece of spruce framing. There are a few that are shaped, ready to be sanded and varnished. And there is Burke's demonstration paddle, signed and dated to remind me of that summer day when I was blown away by the accomplishment of tools in the hand of a craftsman with an eye to make something of utility and grace.

Choosing the Right Wood

The best wood for paddles will be stiff, strong and lightweight. Maple or ash are fine for structure, but they are a bit heavy for long use on the water. Spruce is lighter and easier to shape. Sitka spruce is acclaimed, and rightly so, for being strong and light. But the effort required to secure that species is quite unnecessary.

There is a classification of construc-

tion framing called SPF, which stands for spruce-pine-fir (in this case "hem fir" or "western hemlock"). All three species designated for this class will work in paddle-making. Black spruce is most prevalent, and perhaps the best of the three. Pine has more flex, while hemlock is a little more difficult to work with hand tools.

The wide availability of residential framing stock at a reasonable price is one of the attractive aspects of this project. What is essential is straightness of grain, followed by clear lengths free of knots. Spruce is bedeviled by small knots, and an occasional pin knot will not significantly affect the paddle. I use a drop of cyanoacrylate glue (such as Hot Stuff) to seal small imperfections.

While you need only a 2x6 plank that is 6' long, you are unlikely to find the best lumber in small sizes of framing stock. The longer (16' to 24') and the wider (10" or 12") the stick, the better luck you will have getting your clear paddle blank. I believe this is because the mills use the better grade of logs for the longest lengths, resulting in some portion of a long joist (in a house) being clear. Buy the long length, cut your paddle blanks from the best portion and use the rest of the wood for some future project.

Ten Steps to Making a Paddle

Briefly, here is how the process works: Plane the plank to 1¼" thickness. Trace and cut the silhouette. Block plane and spokeshave all the sides smooth.

Draw lines around the edges to define the center of the paddle and its thicknesses. Thin the paddle's blade using a drawknife and a plane. Shape the handle using a hand saw, drawknife, chisel and plane.

Round the shaft by first making it an octagon. Transition the shaft to the blade and handle with a spokeshave. Smooth the paddle, with a wood rasp and sandpaper. And finally, varnish the paddle leaving the grip unfinished.

Creating a Paddle Blank

Plane your plank to 1¼" thick. Then draw the silhouette of your paddle. It's easiest to trace around an existing paddle, making adjustments in shaft length to fit the intended paddler's height. Paddle length is a personal matter—generally, the paddle should be about chin height.

To follow the plans given at right, start by making a centerline the length of the plank. Next, mark off both ends of the paddle. Mark where the blade and shaft meet, the start of the handle, and the saw kerf on the grip. (See the photo above for details.) Now mark half-widths (use the widths given on the drawing divided in half) on either side of the centerline for the blade at its narrower and wider parts, the shaft and the grip. Then connect your marks to outline the paddle. Use a straightedge for the main lines and sketch in the curved parts.

Cut out the paddle blank on the band saw as shown above. Use a block plane to smooth and fair the edges. Check your work by holding the paddle at arm's length to see if you have a fair outline.

Spokeshave-friendly Project

You will need a spokeshave to smooth the hollows. There will be several places where this traditional tool comes in handy, mostly at transitions from one shape to another. These transitions can be troublesome. You could use a variety of rasps and sanders, but the traditional spokeshave is the tool of choice.

According to some historical accounts, the spokeshave got its name from its use in transitioning wheel

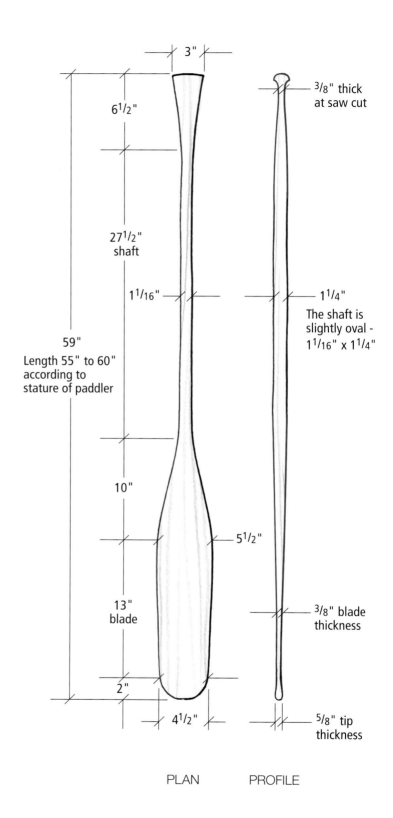

PLAN   PROFILE

ILLUSTRATIONS BY MATT BANTLY

spokes from the square hub end to the round section. You will find this tool indispensable for making the transition from the handle to the shaft and from the shaft to the blade.

It is worth your time to buy an effective spokeshave. Because of the absence of wooden wheels these days, a good spokeshave is hard to find. Therefore, they've fallen into disuse—many craftsmen have become frustrated having used bad ones.

You will need a spokeshave with a slight curve to the sole, not a flat one. Some of the best ones are the traditional wood-handled types with a blade flat to the sole, sometimes called razor-type spokeshaves. Another useful spokeshave has a concave sole, which makes it ideal for rounding the shaft of the paddle.

Defining the Paddle's Shape

It is important that the shaft be rounded last because as long as it remains square, you can capture it in the bench vise as you shape both ends of your paddle.

When the silhouette is fair and smooth, trace a centerline on the edge of the blank all around your paddle. Next, trace lines on the edge to show the ⅜" blade thickness, the octagonal edges of the shaft and the location and depth of the cut for the saw kerf at the grip. The profile view on page 162 gives you these lines.

The photo (bottom left on page 164) shows me tracing a centerline using the woodworker's method—a pencil held effectively between the fingers. If you haven't done this before, give it some practice. It is a great time-saving tip that

shows off your skill as a craftsman. See page 167 for more details.

Thin the blade to ⅜" using the drawknife to rough it out and plane it smooth. Burke leaves the tip of the blade about ⅝" thick, which is something that I like. This strengthens the end, which is vulnerable to being cracked.

Shape the handle by first sawing a kerf across the paddle 1½" from the end to a depth that leaves ⅜" in the center. Then drawknife away the wood for 5" along the shaft to meet your cut line. Chisel the handle to meet the cut line. I like to chisel a hollowed cut for a good finger grip.

Round the end with a block plane and use a wood rasp (a toothed file) for finishing touches as shown in the drawing on page 168.

Layout involves transferring the dimensions from the plans. The centerline with cross lines indicate the major points. Connect the straight lines, then sketch in the curved transitions.

After planing the plank to 1¼" thick, band saw the paddle blank to shape.

The shaft is made slightly oval using a bench plane to first reduce it to an octagon. This will keep it uniform when planing the smaller edges smooth with a block plane and a curved spokeshave.

Use the spokeshave to shape the transition from the shaft to the blade. This versatile tool works equally well pulling or pushing so you can follow the change in grain direction.

Sanding and varnishing completes the paddle. Traditionally, a canoe paddle's handle is left unfinished to give you a better grip on the wood.

I have spent many enjoyable days paddling a canoe with a traditional paddle such as this. Making paddles for your children appropriate to their height is especially meaningful for a parent introducing offspring to the water.

Smooth all the paddle's edges with a block plane. If any lines don't look fair to you, planing can make them so.

Using your pencil held as shown, trace a centerline on all edges.

Use a drawknife to rough the blade to thickness. Bevel the edges first as shown, then take down the center. It may be tough using this tool, so try to hold it the way the photo shows. This should ease the struggle a bit.

Use the bench plane to smooth the blade to its final ⅜" thickness. The pencil lines on the edge should give you guidance in this step.

The point of the blade is left thicker (⅝") to reinforce the point where splits are possible.

Saw down to a point on the handle, leaving ⅜" for the grip.

The drawknife removes waste as you approach the saw kerf at the handle.

3 Traditional Hand Tools Plus 1 Hand Skill

Tools solve problems in wood. Hand tools bought just to collect do not serve you well. But tools bought when you need them will serve many projects to come. Don't hesitate to buy a good hand tool suitable to the task. The tools mentioned here actually stand a chance of being useful in the hands of some future woodworker a century from now.

Drawknife

I owned a drawknife for years without ever putting it to use. There were only two instances when I observed it being used in the hands of a professional. One was in a boat shop where planks along the sheer (the top of the sides where it meets the deck) were being finished off in the gentle curve that makes the profile of the hull. The other was watching Geoff Burke make a paddle that fine summer day. I have since learned that there are several styles and blade treatments for this tool.

Drawknives are made in a variety of sizes for a variety of tasks. The largest drawknife is used for peeling bark from logs. Carvers' drawknives are small. The one shown in this article is referred to as a carpenter's drawknife, and is 12" long with a 7"-wide blade.

As is so often true, the critical point of this tool is the sharpness and angle of the blade. Hogging off rough chunks of wood is not light work. Check the angle of sharpening before use. The tools often are made with an angle of 25° to 30°, which is steeper than necessary and will make heavy going of your work. A finer pitch of 15° to 20° will serve well in the straight-grained softwood of a paddle.

Drawknives are used bevel up for straight cuts. Turned over they will follow contours for shaping. Leonard Lee, in his book "The Complete Guide to Sharpening" (Taunton Press), points to an alternative:

"If you put a 15° basic bevel on a drawknife and dub [a slight bevel on the flat side] from 2° to 5° off the face of the knife, you will find that it is much more maneuverable." (See the drawing of a modified drawknife at right.)

Old drawknives of good quality can still be found at a considerable savings, and they can give you great satisfaction for having rescued a very useful tool.

For a new drawknife contact Ray Larsen, author of "Tool Making for Woodworkers" (Cambium Press). He has been forging quality tools for more than 30 years. Call 781-826-8931 or visit windsorchairresources.com.

Spokeshave

This is a short-soled plane used for smoothing hollows that typically appear when transitioning from one shape to another.

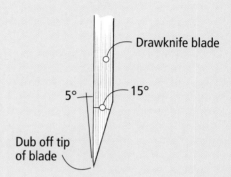

Drawknife blade
5°   15°
Dub off tip of blade

Modern versions of the spokeshave have a metal body holding the blade at an angle to the sole similar to a plane. They come with a flat sole like a conventional plane for flat work or outside curves, with a convex curved sole for shaving inside curves, or with a concave sole. Two high-quality versions of this concave-soled tool should be available from Veritas (Lee Valley Tools, 800-871-8158 or leevalley.com) and Lie-Nielsen Toolworks (800-327-2520 or lie-nielsen.com) by the time you read this.

The traditional spokeshave had a wood body and the blade lying flat to the sole. They are sometimes called razor-type shaves, identifying the shape of the blade, which looks like a traditional straight razor. The change in blade angle makes the modern version less effective for many cutting operations. The flat position of the razor-type blade makes it easy to work with.

The traditional wood-bodied shaves have a 6° to 8° bevel in the sole ahead of the cutting edge. This allows for making hollows, while the blade slices into the wood at no angle at all. (Check out the "Tool Reviews" link at popwood.com or see the April 2004 issue of *Popular Woodworking* for a review of metal-bodied spokeshaves, and the November 2003 issue for information about traditional wood-bodied razor-type spokeshaves.)

Following are sources for spokeshaves:

- Dave Wachnicki (603-356-8712 or ncworkshops.com) has been making shaves for chairmakers in the traditional design.

- Glen Livingstone (508-669-5245 or woodjoytools.com) makes

small, medium and large shaves. The largest is especially favored by boatbuilders.

- Leonard Lee of Lee Valley Tools not only wrote a great book on sharpening, he has pioneered a new generation of spokeshaves under the Veritas label, including metal-bodied shaves with flat, curved and concave soles.

- High-quality metal shaves also are available from Lie-Nielsen Toolworks.

Block Plane

For years, a block plane was a familiar tool tucked into my nail apron as a trim carpenter. It was used for almost any planing job, not just the smoothing of end grain that tradition has made its appointed task. To this day, I will reach for a block plane more often than a bench plane to smooth wood.

Fortunately, a good version of this plane, the Stanley No. 60½, is readily available. You will find this version in most tool catalogs and may even find it in the hardware section of a home-supply store.

Be aware that there are two versions of the block plane—a regular and a low-angle. The low-angle Stanley No. 60½ is ¼" narrower than the standard version. It is this low-angle, narrower block plane that fits my hand best.

In all these tools, their effectiveness depends on being sharp. That should be job one before beginning your paddle.

While your forefinger and thumb grasp the pencil, your middle finger or ring finger acts as an edge stop to define the width of the line.

Finger Marking Gauge

To the list of these tools—drawknife, spokeshave and block plane—I have added a fourth "tool:" the finger marking gauge. This is simply a pencil in your hand.

I learned this skill from my father so early in my woodworking career that I thought everyone knew how to do it. That is, until I started teaching woodworking. I would use this technique for gauging a line along a board and find that my students would do a double-take to see where the straight line came from.

The photo below shows this better than a description could. The middle or ring finger serves as a stop to determine the width of the space to be drawn. To find the center of a board, as in the paddle blank, simply gauge a line from both sides approximately half the board's width. Seeing now how closely they meet in the center gives you an eye for the exact center to set the final holding position for your finger marking gauge. In applications where the space to the gauge line widens, you need to hold the pencil higher, using your ring finger instead of your middle finger as a stop.

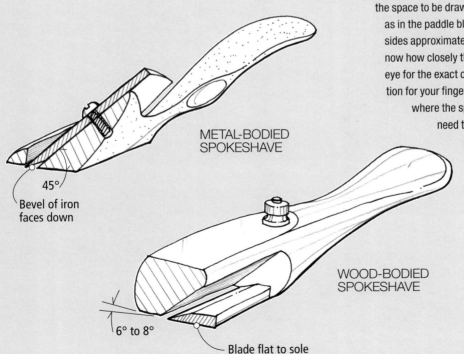

METAL-BODIED SPOKESHAVE

45°
Bevel of iron faces down

WOOD-BODIED SPOKESHAVE

6° to 8°

Blade flat to sole

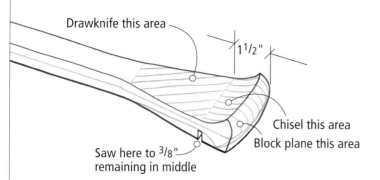

Drawknife this area

1¹/₂"

Chisel this area

Block plane this area

Saw here to ³/₈" remaining in middle

A block plane will round over a comfortable end. The profile shows well here.

The shaft is planed into an octagon following guide lines.

Chisel a hollow approaching the saw kerf. Beware that two cut lines like this can be difficult to blend smoothly. Before cutting too far, expect to clean it up with a rasp and sandpaper.

The block plane will quickly smooth all the edges into a $^{11}/_{16}$" x 1¼" oval, as I'm doing here.

The spokeshave (I'm using a wooden one here) is used to smooth the transition between blade, shaft and handle. It works pulling or pushing to follow the direction of the grain.

A spokeshave with a concave sole, such as this one from Veritas, excels at rounding the shaft of the paddle.

Potting Bench

BY JOHN MARCKWORTH

Behind every serious gardener there's usually a serious potting bench. This outdoor work station sees year-round use—from starting seeds in the spring, to repotting and through fall and wintercleanup.

Potting benches are sometimes available at garden centers and through specialty catalogs, but my impression is that they're usually pretty light-duty. The design I've developed is more industrial-strength than boutique but it has a bit of style thrown in for good measure.

Supplies

No. 8 × 1¼" (30mm) outdoor-rated pocket-hole screws

No. 8 × 2" (50mm) deck screws

No. 8 × 2" (50mm) outdoor-rated washer-head screws

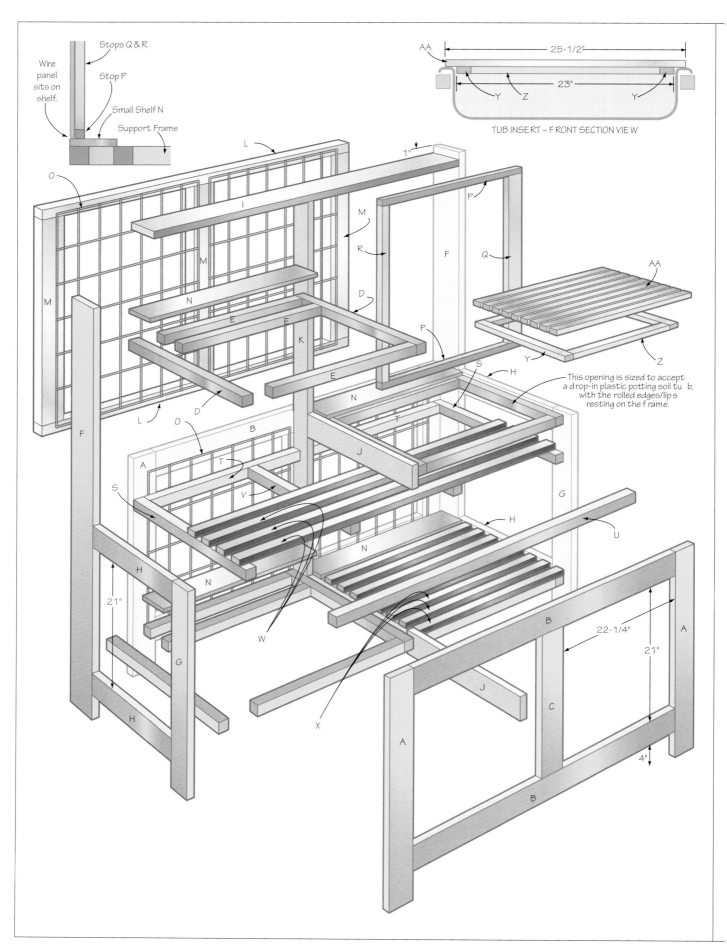

Wire panel sits on shelf.

Stops Q & R

Stop P

Small Shelf N

Support Frame

AA

25-1/2"

23"

Y Z Y

TUB INSERT – FRONT SECTION VIEW

L

1"

I

O

M

M

P

M

R

F

Q

D

AA

N

F

E E

Q

K

D

D

L

E

P

P

N

S H

Y

Z

This opening is sized to accept a drop-in plastic potting soil tub, with the rolled edges/lips resting on the frame.

F

L

O

B

T

J

H

A

S

T

G

V

N

U

H

N

W

S

B

H

H

21"

G

N

X

A

22-1/4"

21"

J

C

A

4"

B

Schedule of Materials: Potting Bench

LTR.	NO.	ITEM	STOCK	INCHES T	(MM) T	INCHES W	(MM) W	INCHES L	(MM) L	COMMENTS
A	4	outside stiles	5/4×4 cedar	1	(25)	3½	(89)	32	(813)	
B	4	top & bottom rails	5/4×4 cedar	1	(25)	3½	(89)	48	(1219)	
C	2	center stiles	5/4×4 edar	1	(25)	3½	(89)	21	(533)	
D	8	outside frame pieces	2×2 cedar	1½	(25)	1½	(25)	25	(635)	
E	12	inside frame pieces	2×2cedar	1½	(25)	1½	(25)	24	(610)	
F	2	back vertical frame pieces	5/4×6 cedar	1	(25)	5½	(140)	68	(1727)	
G	2	front vertical frame pieces	5/4×4 cedar	1	(25)	3½	(89)	32	(813)	
H	4	side horiz. frame pieces	5/4×4 cedar	1	(25)	3½	(89)	19	(483)	
I	1	top shelf	5/4×6 cedar	1	(25)	5½	(140)	55	(1397)	
J	1	lower horiz. frame piece	5/4×4 cedar	1	(25)	3½	(89)	21½	(546)	
K	2	back cntr vert frame piece	5/4×4 cedar	1	(25)	3½	(89)	58½	(1486)	
L	2	top & bottom rails	5/4×2 cedar	1	(25)	1½	(38)	55	(1397)	
M	3	stiles	5/4×4 cedar	1	(25)	3½	(89)	31	(787)	
N	4	small back shelves	5/4×6 cedar	1	(25)	4⅜	(111)	27	(686)	
O	4	wire mesh panels	steel	N/A		N/A				galvanized steel wire fence 4" (102mm), cut to fit
P	8	horizontal stops	5/4×5/4 cedar	1	(25)	1	(25)	27	(686)	
Q	4	outside vertical stops	5/4×3 cedar	1	(25)	2½	(64)	CTF		cut to fit
R	4	inside vertical stops	5/4×5/4 cedar	1	(25)	1	(25)	CTF		cut to fit
S	2	side frame pieces	2×2 cedar	1½	(25)	1½	(25)	25	(635)	
T	2	back frame pieces	2×2 cedar	1½	(25)	1½	(25)	25½	(648)	
U	1	front frame piece	2×2 cedar	1½	(25)	1½	(25)	55	(1397)	
V	2	intermediate frame pieces	2×2 cedar	1½	(25)	1½	(25)	22	(559)	
W	8	upper shelf slats	1×2 cedar	¾	(19)	1½	(25)	55	(1397)	
X	20	lower shelf slats	1×2 cedar	¾	(19)	1½	(25)	26¾	(679)	
Y	4	frame stiles	1×2 cedar	¾	(19)	1½	(25)	17	(432)	
Z	4	frame rails	1×2 cedar	¾	(19)	1½	(25)	20	(508)	
AA	18	tub cover slats	1×2 cedar	¾	(19)	1½	(25)	25½	(648)	
BB	1	upper horiz. frame piece	5/4×4 cedar	1	(25)	3½	(89)	25	(635	

Planning and Layout

The starting point for my design was the work top. I wanted a traditional slat surface, but I also wanted tub containers that could hold potting soil. In the end I combined these design elements into two framed openings that could accept either a slat insert or a plastic tub. I found a plastic tub I liked at a farm supply store and adjusted the construction dimensions to its measurements, but it would be easy to change the layout to fit another tub size.

I chose to use dimensional lumber whenever possible to keep costs down, and also to make construction easier. The main frame components are made from 5/4 tight-knot (TK) cedar decking, which comes with all four edges rounded over. The tub/slat insert support frames are made from 2×2 clear cedar, and the slats are 1×2 clear cedar. All screws and fasteners are outdoor/deck-rated. There's no fancy joinery or glue joints in the construction—just a straight-ahead, no-frills design.

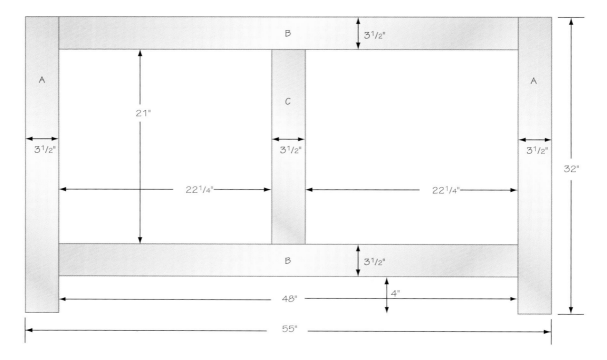

STEP ONE Using outdoor-rated pocket-hole screws, assemble the identical front and lower back face frames ABC.

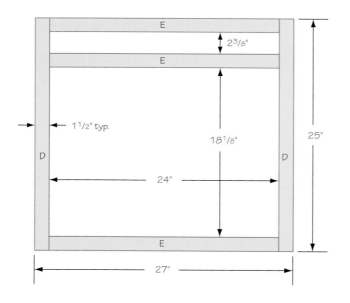

STEP TWO Using 2×2 cedar and 2" (50mm) deck screws, begin by building four identical support frames DE: two for the top surface to house the tubs or slat inserts, and two more for the bottom slat shelves.

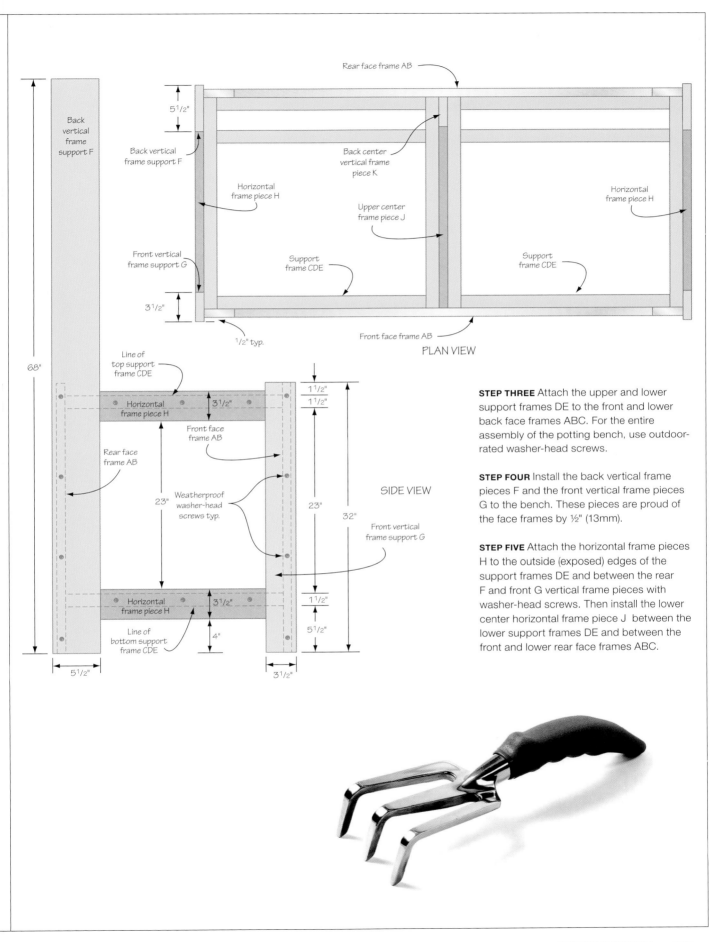

Rear face frame AB

Back
vertical
frame
support F

5¹/₂"

Back vertical
frame support F

Back center
vertical frame
piece K

Horizontal
frame piece H

Horizontal
frame piece H

Upper center
frame piece J

Front vertical
frame support G

Support
frame CDE

Support
frame CDE

3¹/₂"

68"

¹/₂" typ.

Front face frame AB

PLAN VIEW

Line of
top support
frame CDE

1¹/₂"
1¹/₂"

Horizontal
frame piece H

3¹/₂"

Front face
frame AB

Rear face
frame AB

SIDE VIEW

23"

Weatherproof
washer-head
screws typ.

23"

32"

Front vertical
frame support G

Horizontal
frame piece H

3¹/₂"

1¹/₂"

Line of
bottom support
frame CDE

4"

5¹/₂"

5¹/₂"

3¹/₂"

STEP THREE Attach the upper and lower support frames DE to the front and lower back face frames ABC. For the entire assembly of the potting bench, use outdoor-rated washer-head screws.

STEP FOUR Install the back vertical frame pieces F and the front vertical frame pieces G to the bench. These pieces are proud of the face frames by ½" (13mm).

STEP FIVE Attach the horizontal frame pieces H to the outside (exposed) edges of the support frames DE and between the rear F and front G vertical frame pieces with washer-head screws. Then install the lower center horizontal frame piece J between the lower support frames DE and between the front and lower rear face frames ABC.

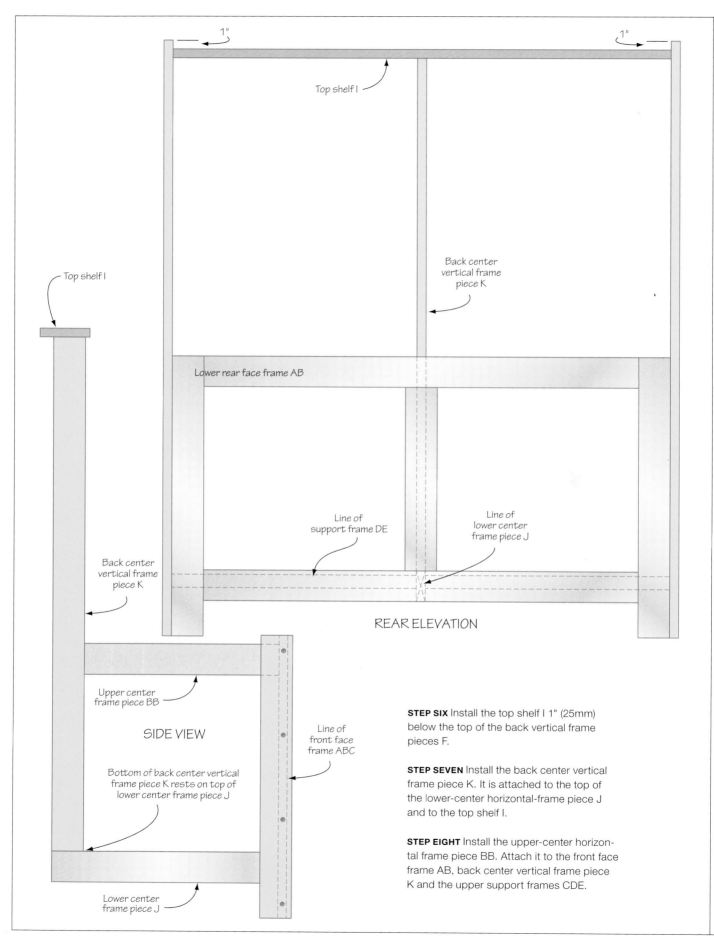

1"

1"

Top shelf I

Back center
vertical frame
piece K

Lower rear face frame AB

Line of
support frame DE

Line of
lower center
frame piece J

REAR ELEVATION

Top shelf I

Back center
vertical frame
piece K

Upper center
frame piece BB

SIDE VIEW

Line of
front face
frame ABC

Bottom of back center vertical
frame piece K rests on top of
lower center frame piece J

Lower center
frame piece J

STEP SIX Install the top shelf I 1" (25mm) below the top of the back vertical frame pieces F.

STEP SEVEN Install the back center vertical frame piece K. It is attached to the top of the lower-center horizontal-frame piece J and to the top shelf I.

STEP EIGHT Install the upper-center horizontal frame piece BB. Attach it to the front face frame AB, back center vertical frame piece K and the upper support frames CDE.

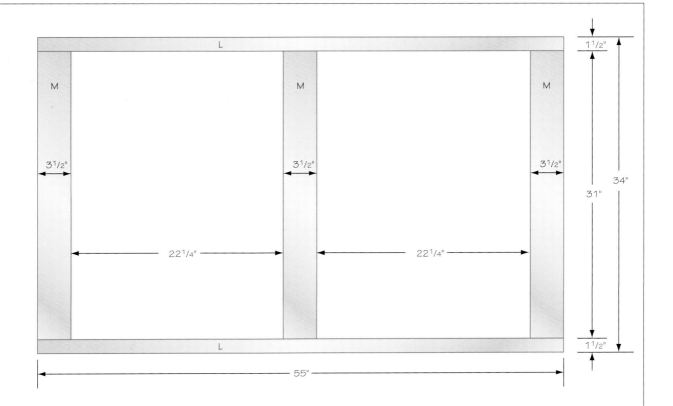

STEP NINE Attach the upper rear face-frame parts in place.

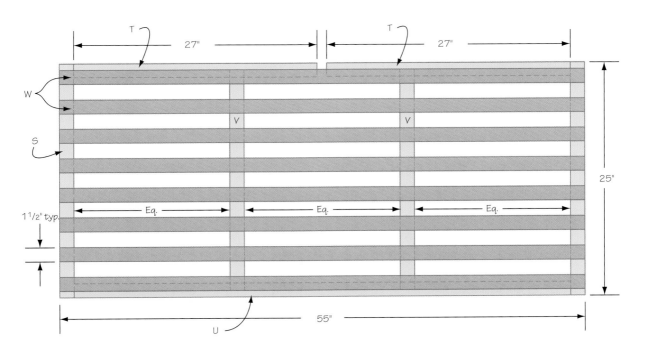

STEP TEN Assemble the upper slat shelf STUVW. This shelf supports the bottoms of the tubs.

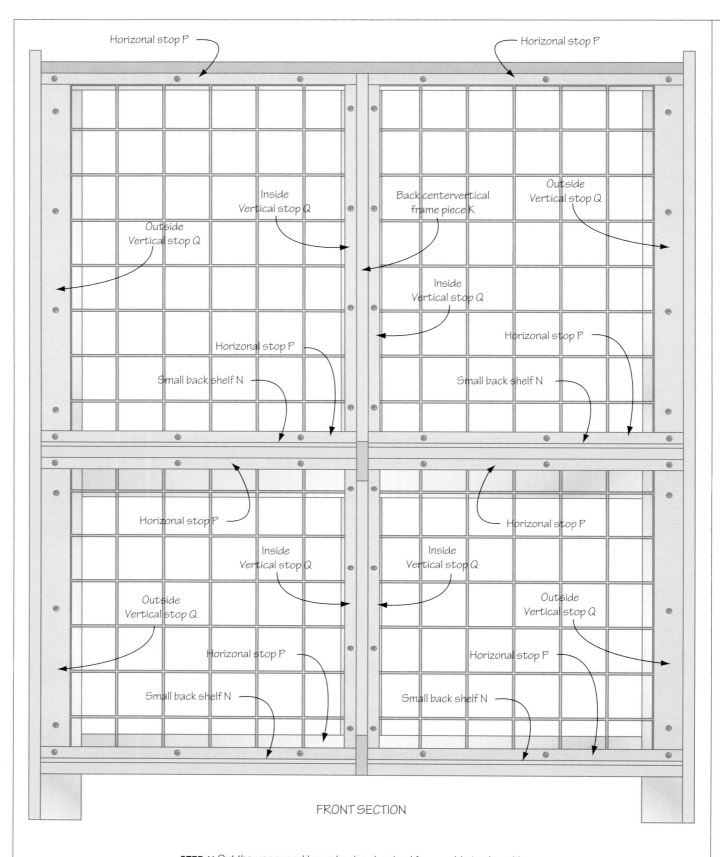

Horizonal stop P

Horizonal stop P

Inside
Vertical stop Q

Back centervertical
frame piece K

Outside
Vertical stop Q

Outside
Vertical stop Q

Inside
Vertical stop Q

Horizonal stop P

Horizonal stop P

Small back shelf N

Small back shelf N

Horizonal stop P

Horizonal stop P

Inside
Vertical stop Q

Inside
Vertical stop Q

Outside
Vertical stop Q

Outside
Vertical stop Q

Horizonal stop P

Horizonal stop P

Small back shelf N

Small back shelf N

FRONT SECTION

STEP 11 Cut the upper and lower back galvanized fence grids to size with bolt cutters and install them using wood stops against the upper and lower back face frames. I chose this grid material because it's completely weatherproof, is open, lets light through and makes a great place to hang tools, watering cans and so forth.

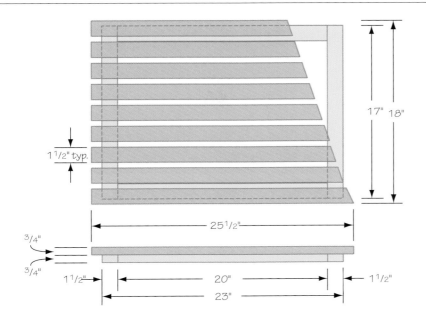

17" 18"

1 1/2" typ.

25 1/2"

3/4"

3/4"

1 1/2"

20"

1 1/2"

23"

STEP 12 Assemble the tubs inserts. These inserts provide a work surface that will let potting soil or whatever fall between the slats and land in the tub below.

STEP 13 I didn't apply any finish or sealer to the potting bench. I chose to let the cedar naturally turn to a weathered gray color. I did, however, soak the bottoms of the corner frame pieces in sealer where they rest on the ground.

Gravity Feeder

BY A. J. HAMLER

Schedule of Materials: Cottage

LTR.	NO.	ITEM	STOCK	INCHES T	(MM) T	INCHES W	(MM) W	INCHES L	(MM) L	COMMENTS
A	2	ends	cedar	¾	(19)	6¾	(171)	7¼	(184))	blank size before cutting to shape
B	1	bottom	cedar	¾	(19)	4½	(114)	7½	(191)	
C	2	tray sides	cedar	¾	(19)	1½	(38)	9	(229)	
D	2	roof halves	cedar	¾	(19)	5	(127)	11	(279)	
E	2	spacers	hardwood	½	(13)	½	(13)	4½	(114)	
F	2	windows	acrylic	⅛	(3)	4	(102)	8	(203)	
G	1	continuous hinge	brass					10½	(267)	

Using a tried-and-true design, gravity feeders can hold a large amount of chow. The wide opening at the bottom accommodates a seed mix containing everything from large sunflower seeds to tiny millet seed.

With its clear sides, it's easy to see when it's time to refill. (Of course, all of your birds suddenly disappearing is another good clue the feeder's empty.) The version here features a hinged roof, making refilling a quick task. We'll use ¾" cedar for this project, with ⅛" acrylic for the windows.

Begin by laying out the end pattern on your workpiece, as in Fig. 1. Note that the end pattern has straight sides, with a curved line inside the outer edges. (We'll cut that curve out later, but the straight edges are necessary for first cutting slots to accommodate the windows.) I used the band saw to cut the end patterns, but you can also use a jigsaw or handsaw. Choose the orientation you want for the end pieces and use a pencil to mark the inside faces.

Cut the slots for the windows on the table saw. Set the fence at 1", and raise the blade to cut a ¼"-deep slot in a single pass, as in Fig. 3. Once the slots are cut, there's no need for that straight edge any longer, so layout and cut the waste from the curved edges. A spindle sander works great to smooth the inside curve. (Fig. 4)

Put a bit of glue on each end of the bottom and nail the ends in place. (Fig.

5) Attach the window spacers at the inside corners with glue and a pair of brads. This spacer will set the height of the side windows, creating a gap at the bottom of each to allow seeds to flow into the feeding tray. These spacers can be made of any weather-resistant wood, and I happened to have some ½" × ½" oak scrap, so I used that. With the spacers in place, attach the tray sides with glue and nails, as in Fig. 6.

Cut the windows to size and test-fit them in the slots as in Fig. 7. Note that I've left the protective film in place on the acrylic. When working with acrylic or other plastic sheets, leave this film in place as long as possible to prevent scratching the plastic while you work.

The roof is made in identical halves, joined in the middle with a continuous hinge (sometimes called a piano hinge). I've found that it's easiest to make and hinge the roof before attaching it to the main part of the feeder. Cut the roof halves to size, and cut a 60° bevel along one edge of each half.

The hinge you get will undoubtedly be too long, so you'll need to cut it to length. You can use a hacksaw for this, or a rotary tool with a cutting disk if you have one. It's not necessary, by the way,

for the hinge to run the entire length of the roof. In fact, depending on the hinge you get, it may be difficult to cut it to the exact roof length since the hinges are already drilled—the exact roof length may place screw holes too close to the ends, inviting split-out when driving the screws. The hinge I used here is cut about ¼" short of the roof length on each end to center the holes in the hinge.

Center the hinge on one beveled edge to mark for the screw holes. I used an awl to create some small pilot holes as shown in Fig. 8., but you can also drill them. Cedar is very soft and easily takes screws, but pilot holes eliminate the chance of splitting the wood. Butt the other roof half up against the hinge of the first half, and attach it the same way.

Lay the completed roof on top of the main portion of the feeder to check for fit, and mark one side in pencil, as shown in Fig. 9, to help you accurately place the nails. (I've made my pencil lines very dark for photo purposes, but make your marks as light as possible for easier removal.) Put a bit of glue on the top edges of one side of the feeder, and nail the roof in place on that side. Be sure you have the window in place on that side before nailing. Give the feeder a good sanding to remove any pencil marks and to ease any sharp edges.

Simply flip open one side of the roof to fill. The best seed to use for a gravity feeder of this type is a mixed seed, which will attract the greatest variety of birds. Several mixes are available that are designed to attract specific species, so the choice is yours.

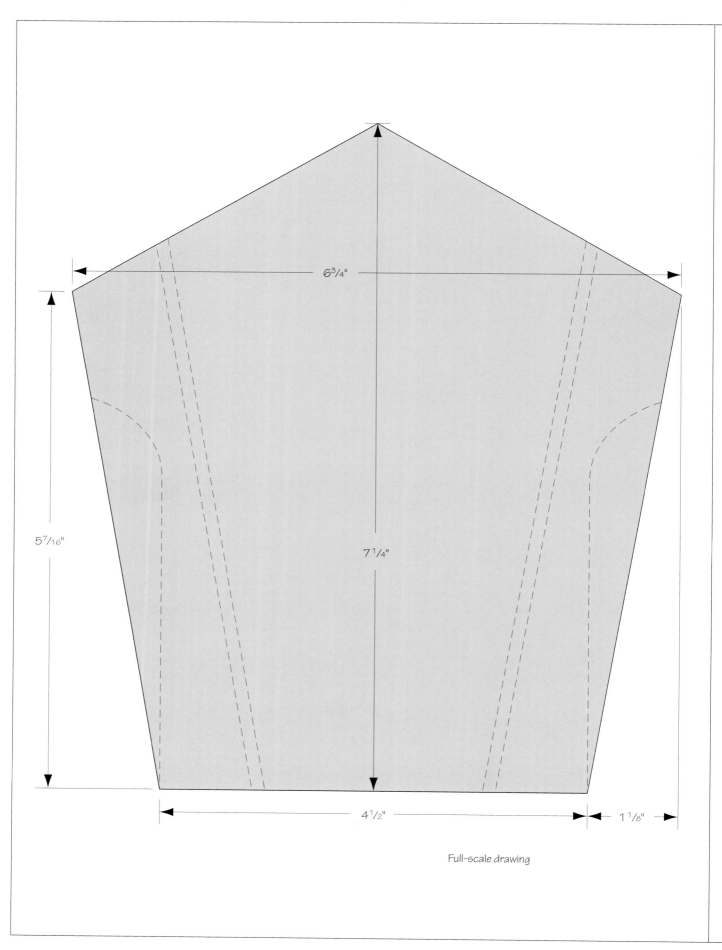

6³/₄"

7¹/₄"

5⁷/₁₆"

4¹/₂"

1¹/₈"

Full-scale drawing

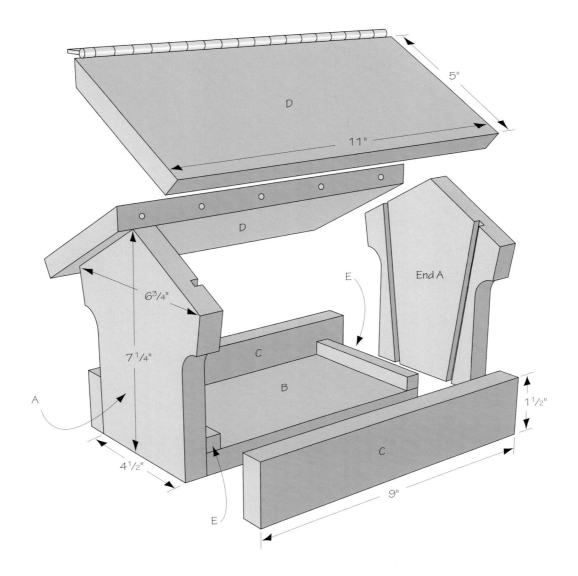

FIGURE 1 Make a full-sized pattern of the end and use it to trace the shape on the workpiece.

FIGURE 2 Use a band saw or jigsaw to cut out the ends.

FIGURE 3 Use the table saw to cut the slots for the acrylic panels.

FIGURE 4 An oscillating spindle sander does a good job sanding the curves.

FIGURE 5 Glue and nail the ends to the bottom.

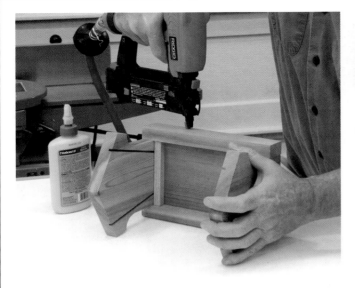

FIGURE 6 Attach the tray sides with glue and nails.

FIGURE 7 Fit the acrylic to the feeder, *then* remove the covering.

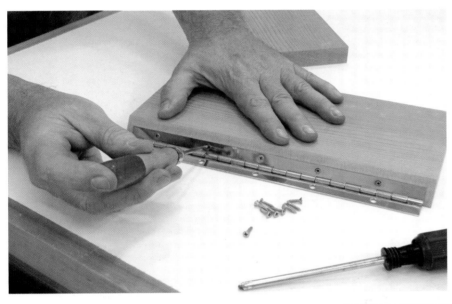

FIGURE 8 Use an awl to mark the screw holes. Cedar is soft enough for you to screw into without drilling, but pilot holes are recommended to prevent splitting the wood.

FIGURE 9 Lightly draw (mine are dark so you can see them in the photo) locating lines on the roof sections, then glue and nail the roof in place.

Hummingbird Feeder

BY A. J. HAMLER

Of all the birds you may want to attract to your yard, the hummingbird is one of the most fascinating to watch. Almost defying nature with the speed of their wings, you won't regret inviting them to your home.

Faster than a speeding bullet barely describes hummingbirds, among the tiniest birds you can attract to a feeder. How tiny? The typical ruby-throated hummingbird, one of the most common, weighs in at about 3 grams, or about $1/10$ of an ounce. They can zip in and out of a feeder at lighting speed with their wings all but invisible, and no wonder—the typical ruby-throat beats its wings about 50 times per second (3,000 times a minute!). This wing speed and agility make the hummingbird the only bird that can fly backward.

Hummingbirds subsist almost entirely on nectar, and many prefer the nectar of red, orange or pink flowers. For feeders, sugar water—often colored red—is their favorite. This feeder, made of ¾" cedar, features twin tubes of liquid so more than one bird can feed at a time. (If the first one at the feeder allows it, that is; the first one there often chases newcomers away.)

You can use almost any kind of tube, but 1"-diameter test tubes or watering tubes (of the kind used for household birds and other pets, which I've used here) are the easiest to find. Almost any bird supplier carries rubber stoppers and angled feeding tubes that fit a 1" test tube. Look for feeding tubes that include a small cap on the end, pierced with a tiny hole in the center.

Begin by cutting feeder components to size and shape. Because the top and bottom are identical, it's easiest to cut and drill them simultaneously. Join a pair of slightly oversized workpieces together by driving small nails into the corners, and then transfer the top/bottom pattern to the top workpiece. When drilling, you want to drill all the way through the top piece but only halfway through the bottom, so set your drill press depth stop so it only goes about ⅜" into the bottom piece. (Fig. 1) Now move to the band saw and cut out the two pieces as in Fig. 2. With the top and bottom cut out and separated, sand both oval workpieces as needed to smooth the shapes. In the bottom piece, drill a $7/16$" hole in the center of each of the larger holes. This hole-within-a-hole will support the bottoms of the test tubes, but allow the smaller feeding tube to go through the bottom of the feeder. You can see this piece in the foreground of Fig. 3.

Attach the 1½" sides to the center workpiece as in Fig. 3, resulting in an H-shaped assembly. Center the feeder bottom—large holes facing the center assembly—and glue and nail in place as in Fig. 4.

With the feeder still inverted, center the feeder on the top piece and pencil a mark centered and up against the sides of the center assembly exactly as with the suet feeder in the previous chapter. This is where the wire hanger will pass through. Make a similar centered mark about 1" from the top of each side. Using a bit that matches the thickness of your wire hanger, drill holes on the marks in the feeder top and on each side of the feeder.

Just as with the hanger on the suet feeder, bend the hanger wire into a curved shape and slip the ends through the holes you drilled into the top, and make a 90° bend in the tip of each wire oriented inward. Slip the angled ends into the holes in the feeder sides.

Thread the narrow angled feeder tubes through the holes in the bottom then, holding the tubes in place with one hand, slide the top down over both tubes so they fit through the holes in the top, as in Fig. 5.

Since hummingbirds migrate during the winter you'll probably want to bring the feeder in for cleaning and storage, but here's another use for it. Store the stoppers and their angled feeder tubes where you'll find them easily when spring returns. Now reverse the two test tubes open-end up. Fill the tubes with water and your hummingbird feeder serves nicely as a small flower vase.

Schedule of Materials: Hummingbird Feeder

LTR.	NO.	ITEM	STOCK	INCHES T	(MM) T	INCHES W	(MM) W	INCHES L	(MM) L
A	1	top	cedar	¾	(19)	3½	(89)	5¼	(133)
B	1	bottom	cedar	¾	(19)	3½	(89)	5¼	(133)
C	1	center	cedar	¾	(19)	2½	(64)	6	(152)
D	2	center sides	cedar	¾	(19)	1½	(38)	6	(152)
E	1	wire hanger; copper or brass	metal	⅛	3 d			18	(457)

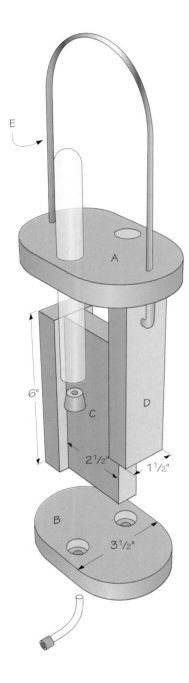

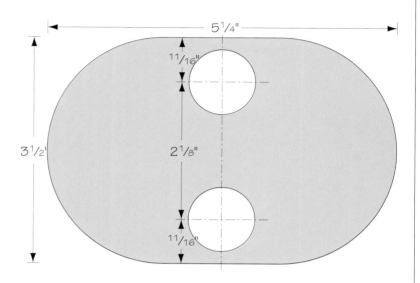

FIGURE 1 Drill all the way through the top piece but only half-way through the bottom.

FIGURE 2 Now cut the top and bottom pieces to shape using the band saw.

A Note About Hummingbirds

Hummingbirds are found throughout the Western Hemisphere (although tropical Central and South America have far more species). Two of the most common species in North America are the ruby-throated, found mostly in the eastern U.S., and the very similar black-chinned, found mostly in the west. They build tiny cuplike nests in trees (sometimes using spider silk as one of the materials), and lay only two or three eggs per brood. Because they feed exclusively on flower nectar, both species migrate to warmer climates in the winter.

FIGURE 3 With glue and nails, attach the 1½" sides to the center piece.

FIGURE 4 Center the feeder bottom and glue and nail it in place.

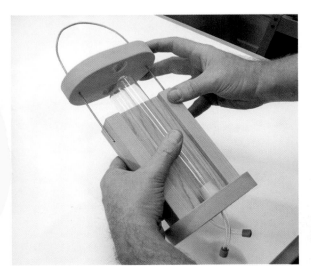

FIGURE 5 Thread the narrow angled feeder tubes through the holes in the bottom. Then, holding the tubes in place with one hand, slide the top down over both tubes so they fit through the holes in the top.

FIGURE 6 Since hummingbirds migrate during the winter you'll probably want to bring the feeder in for cleaning and storage, but here's another use for it—fill the tubes with water and your hummingbird feeder serves nicely as a small flower vase.

Easy-to-Build Outdoor Projects. Copyright © 2012 by F+W Media, Inc. Printed and bound in USA. All rights reserved. No part of this book may be reproduced in any form or by any electronic or mechanical means including information storage and retrieval systems without permission in writing from the publisher, except by a reviewer, who may quote brief passages in a review. Published by Popular Woodworking Books, an imprint of F+W Media, Inc., 10151 Carver Rd., Suite 200, Blue Ash, Ohio, 45242. (800) 289-0963 First edition.

Distributed in Canada by Fraser Direct
100 Armstrong Avenue
Georgetown, Ontario L7G 5S4
Canada

Distributed in the U.K. and Europe by
F&W Media International, LTD
Brunel House, Forde Close
Newton Abbot
TQ12 4PU, UK
Tel: (+44) 1626 323200
Fax: (+44) 1626 323319
E-mail: enquiries@fwmedia.com

Distributed in Australia by Capricorn Link
P.O. Box 704
Windsor, NSW 2756
Australia

Visit our website at www.popularwoodworking.com or our consumer website at www.shopwoodworking.com for more woodworking information projects.

Other fine Popular Woodworking Books are available from your local bookstore or direct from the publisher.

16   15   14   13   5   4   3   2

Acquisitions editor: David Thiel
Designer: Angela Wilcox
Production coordinator: Mark Griffin

READ THIS IMPORTANT SAFETY NOTICE

To prevent accidents, keep safety in mind while you work. Use the safety guards installed on power equipment; they are for your protection.

When working on power equipment, keep fingers away from saw blades, wear safety goggles to prevent injuries from flying wood chips and sawdust, wear hearing protection and consider installing a dust vacuum to reduce the amount of airborne sawdust in your woodshop.

Don't wear loose clothing, such as neckties or shirts with loose sleeves, or jewelry, such as rings, necklaces or bracelets, when working on power equipment. Tie back long hair to prevent it from getting caught in your equipment.

People who are sensitive to certain chemicals should check the chemical content of any product before using it.

Due to the variability of local conditions, construction materials, skill levels, etc., neither the author nor Popular Woodworking Books assumes any responsibility for any accidents, injuries, damages or other losses incurred resulting from the material presented in this book.

The authors and editors who compiled this book have tried to make the contents as accurate and correct as possible. Plans, illustrations, photographs and text have been carefully checked. All instructions, plans and projects should be carefully read, studied and understood before beginning construction.

Prices listed for supplies and equipment were current at the time of publication and are subject to change.

METRIC CONVERSION CHART

to convert	to	multiply by
Inches	Centimeters	2.54
Centimeters	Inches	0.4
Feet	Centimeters	30.5
Centimeters	Feet	0.03
Yards	Meters	0.9
Meters	Yards	1.1

NOW AVAILABLE ON DVD!

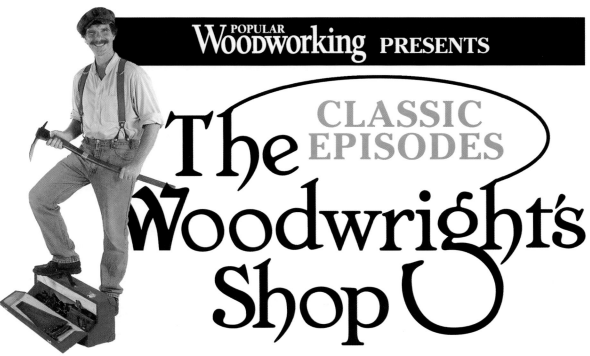

POPULAR Woodworking PRESENTS

The CLASSIC EPISODES Woodwright's Shop

For over 30 years, **Roy Underhill** has been educating and entertaining audiences on *The Woodwright's Shop* with his unrivaled knowledge of traditional hand tools and building techniques. Now, for the first time, these classic episodes are available on DVD. Each 2-disc DVD set includes an entire season, with 6-hours of entertainment. Just want to watch your favorite episodes? All the episodes are also available for streaming straight to your computer.

Bring Roy into your home today!

WWW.POPULARWOODWORKING.COM/ROY-UNDERHILL

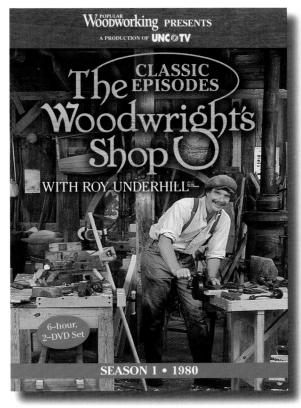

IDEAS. INSTRUCTION. INSPIRATION.

These and other great *Popular Woodworking* products are available at your local bookstore, woodworking store or online supplier.

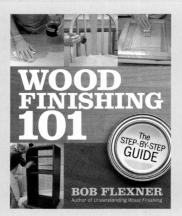

WOOD FINISHING 101
By Bob Flexner

Wood finishing doesn't have to be complicated or confusing. Wood Finishing 101 boils it down to simple step-by-step instructions and pictures on how to finish common woods using widely-available finishing materials. Bob Flexner has been writing about and teaching wood finishing for over 20 years.

paperback • 128 pages

WEEKEND WOODWORKER'S PROJECT COLLECTION

This book has 40 projects from which to choose and, depending on the level of your woodworking skills, any of them can be completed in one or two weekends. Projects include: a game box, jewelry box, several styles of bookcases and shelves, mirrors, picture frames and more.

paperback • 256 pages

POPULAR WOODWORKING MAGAZINE

Whether learning a new hobby or perfecting your craft, *Popular Woodworking Magazine* has expert information to teach the skill, not just the project. Find the latest issue on newsstands, or you can order online at popularwoodworking.com.

SHOPCLASS VIDEOS

From drafting, to dovetails and even how to carve a ball-and-claw foot, our Shop Class Videos let you see the lesson as if you were standing right there.

Available at shopwoodworking.com
DVD & Instant download

POPULAR WOODWORKING'S VIP PROGRAM

Get the Most Out of Woodworking!

Join the Woodworker's Bookshop VIP program today for the tools you need to advance your woodworking abilities. Your one-year paid renewal membership includes:

Popular Woodworking Magazine (1 year/7 issue U.S. subscription — A $21.97 Value)

Popular Woodworking Magazine CD — Get all issues of **Popular Woodworking Magazine** from 2006 to today on one CD (A $64.95 Value!)

The Best of Shops & Workbenches CD — 62 articles on workbenches, shop furniture, shop organization and the essential jigs and fixtures published in **Popular Woodworking** and **Woodworking Magazine** ($15.00 Value!)

20% Members-Only Savings on 6-Month Subscription for Shop Class OnDemand

10% Members-Only Savings at Shopwoodworking.com

10% Members-Only Savings on FULL PRICE Registration for Woodworking In America Conference (Does Not Work with Early Bird Price)

and more....

Visit *popularwoodworking.com* to see more woodworking information by the experts, learn about our digital subscription and sign up to receive our weekly newsletter at *popularwoodworking.com/newsletters/*

Follow Popular Woodworking

BRIDGEPORT PUBLIC LIBRARY

1230244633